An Altitude SuperGuide

Calgary

An Altitude SuperGuide

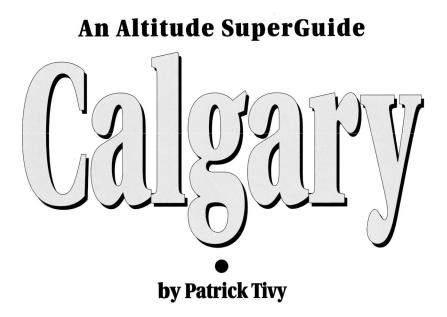

Calgary

by Patrick Tivy

Altitude Publishing Canada Ltd.
Canadian Rockies/Vancouver

Publication Information

Altitude Publishing Canada Ltd.

1500 Railway Avenue, PO Box 1410
Canmore, Alberta T0L 0M0

Copyright 1995 © Altitude
Text Copyright 1995 © Patrick Tivy
Base Map Page 11 Copyright 1994 © Magellan Geographix

Extreme care has been taken to ensure that all information presented in this book is accurate and up-to-date, and neither the author nor the publisher can be held responsible for any errors.

Canadian Cataloguing in Publication Data

Tivy, Patrick, 1945-
  Calgary

(SuperGuide)
Includes index.
ISBN 1-55153-069-4

1. Calgary (Alta.)--Guidebooks. I. Title. II. Series.
FC3697.18.T58 1995   917.123'38043
C94-910970-3   F1079.5.C35T58 1995

Made in Western Canada

Printed and bound in Canada
by Friesen Printers, Altona, Manitoba.

Altitude GreenTree Program

Altitude Publishing will plant in Western Canada twice as many trees as were used in the manufacturing of this product.

Project Development

Concept/Art Direction	Stephen Hutchings
Design	Stephen Hutchings
Editing/Proofreading	Faye Holt
Indexing/Proofreading	Noeline Bridge
Maps	Catherine Burgess
FPO Scanning	Debra Symes
Electronic Page Layout	Sandra Davis,
	Nancy Green,
	Alison Barr
Financial Management	Laurie Smith

A Note from the Publisher

The world described in *Altitude SuperGuides* is a unique and fascinating place. It is a world filled with surprise and discovery, beauty and enjoyment, questions and answers. It is a world of people, cities, landscape, animals and wilderness as seen through the eyes of those who live in, work with, and care for this world. The process of describing this world is also a means of defining ourselves.

It is also a world of relationship, where people derive their meaning from a deep and abiding contact with the land – as well as from each other. And it is this sense of relationship that guides all of us at Altitude to ensure that these places continue to survive and evolve in the decades ahead.

Altitude SuperGuides are books intended to be used, as much as read. Like the world they describe, *Altitude SuperGuides* are evolving, adapting and growing. Please write to us with your comments and observations, and we will do our best to incorporate your ideas into future editions of these books.

Stephen Hutchings
Publisher

Front cover photo: Olympic Saddledome cradles the spectacular Calgary skyline
    Inset: Chuckwagon race
Frontispiece: Cowboys and Calgary, a perfect match
Back cover photo, top: Eau Claire Market
    Below: Heritage Park

Contents

The **Calgary SuperGuide** is organized according to the following colour scheme:

Information and introductory sections ....

Downtown ....

Southeast ....

Southwest ....

Northwest ....

Northeast ....

1. Introduction

The tallest towers in Calgary's downtown business district are occupied by the head offices of Canada's major oil and gas companies

Welcome to Calgary, the friendly city. It's young and boisterous, and seems determined to stay that way, no matter how old and sophisticated it gets. It's a smart city, but Calgarians still like to "horse" around like rowdy teenagers. Calgary has more university graduates per capita than any other city in Canada—149 per thousand, a whopping 25 per cent more than Vancouver—but these well-educated Calgarians choose to amuse themselves each July by dressing up in funny hats and old blue jeans. These intellectuals like to yell, "Yahoo!"

Calgary is famous across the land for its hard-nosed business leaders, but it also has dedicated environmentalists. The community has one of the most spectacular museums in Canada and one of the finest zoos in the world. It's an oil city, yet most of those who work in "the oil patch" rarely see a drop of oil except when they go to a service station. Calgary is the head office for the energy industry, not a production centre. So the oil workers tend to toil in high-rise office towers, not on drilling rigs.

The city has cultivated a wild west cowboy image, but its public library is the busiest in the country. Calgary is supposed to be the heartland of rugged individualism and free enterprise, but its greatest public institution, the Calgary Exhibition & Stampede, simply couldn't exist without the freely-given time of thousands of volunteers.

So many myths about Calgary are just all wrong. People

who don't know the city say, "It's so American!" Yet the city was named after an obscure Scottish bay. The university has a Gaelic motto, and the mayor lives in a neighborhood known as Britannia.

Calgarians have taken their fair share of hard knocks. The local economy has been sent tumbling repeatedly by government policy and international events. Some big established companies have disappeared, but new

The famous white hat is recognized around the world as a symbol of Calgary

ones arise to take their place. Far more often than Calgarians would even want to admit, Calgary's major sports teams have buckled at the last moment and let down the home fans.

Yet Calgarians are not dismayed; they do not dwell on the past. What else would you expect from a city that adopted such an forward-looking motto: Onward.

How to Use the SuperGuide

It's easy to fall in love with Calgary. The natural setting is superb. We are blessed with spectacular scenery in all directions. The sky is clear and blue. The air is fresh. The water is sparkling clean. Best of all, the people are friendly. It's a great place to visit and an even better place to live.

Altitude's *Calgary Super-Guide* follows the same simple principles of organization directing the growth of the city. The first chapters describe the remarkable physical and cul-

tural environment from the earliest days of pioneer settlement.

Many other cities have allowed their downtown cores to deteriorate, but in Calgary, the downtown is still a great place for both business and pleasure. This SuperGuide includes a large section on the downtown attractions, from outstanding examples of architecture to the popular river-bank parks.

Granted a chapter all to itself is the city's most famous attraction. The Calgary Exhibition and Stampede is only 10 days long, but its influence is profound and is felt year-round. The Stampede is a big reason why Calgary isn't like ordinary cities.

From the very beginning, it has been organized in a straight-forward fashion. Until the 1960s, the city was laid out in grid form. Streets run north and south, and avenues go east and west. Most streets and avenues were given numbers instead of names, making

travel very easy. Now, many new residential districts have roads that curve and twist. The roads have fancy names, but even so, one key point has been retained. All addresses in Calgary come complete with a quadrant name. The Super-Guide follows the traditional pattern, starting with Southeast, then proceeding through Southwest, Northwest, and Northeast.

Each quadrant has its own character and chapter. Every address will include the appropriate quadrant identification. SE means Southeast, SW indicates Southwest. The only exceptions are addresses on Centre Street North, and on Macleod Trail South.

Calgary is a city on the move. Numbers change. Businesses move. Restaurants change addresses, owners, chefs, and menus. But all data was accurate at time of publication. If you have comments and suggestions please send them to the author in care of the publisher.

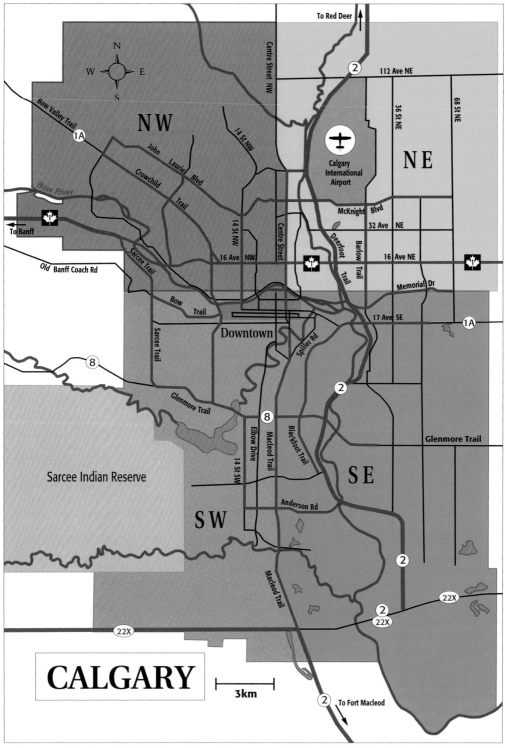

CALGARY

3km

2. Highlights of Nature

Calgary was built in a strategic location in the foothills where the prairies rise to meet the Rocky Mountains

Some things never change. From the beginning of time—at least from the beginning of human activity on the plains ten or twelve thousand years ago—Calgary has been a crossroads. Long before there were highways, railroads, or jet aircraft, travelers were crossing paths here.

The native people who followed the buffalo knew there were ideal grazing areas up and down the valley of the Bow River. The Bow valley has always been a prime entry point into the foothills and mountains.

In the same way, travelers who were headed north or south would make their way to the flat valley floor now occupied by downtown office towers. There the Bow River was wide and shallow, so crossing the swift current was easier than in deeper places.

That made it an important junction on the route archeologists and historians believe extended along the North American continent from Mexico to Alaska.

Today, the tradition continues. Even though regular passenger service has been discontinued, Calgary is a major centre for railroad freight traffic in all directions.

As well, the Calgary International Airport is a hub for freight and passenger flights, and the number of flights by private business jets has made the airport the fourth busiest in the country.

Just as in the days of the buffalo, Calgary is the major intersection where east-west travelers in cars, trucks, and buses cross paths with those headed north or south.

The road traffic meets at a sophisticated layout known to highway engineers as a "double diamond." It's built where Highway 1, the Trans-Canada, meets Highway 2, the main north-south artery in Alberta. Fittingly, the mixed residential and commercial neighborhood surrounding the traffic intersection has a special name, The Crossroads.

In pioneer days, there was good reason to stay at Calgary—good water. Today the Bow and Elbow Rivers provide drinking water rated by public health specialists as among the finest in the world. Modern treatment plants have been built on both rivers, one at the Glenmore Dam on the Elbow and one below the Bearspaw Dam on the Bow.

The high plains of Alberta are dry country. Some regions to the south and east have been classed as semidesert. Rainfall can be very scarce in summer, which has caused recurring problems for farmers. The nomadic hunters, who followed the buffalo, knew there was always good water along the Bow. There were, and still are, many springs that continue to flow, even in the coldest winters, along the valley and in the hills around Calgary.

The coming of the settlers put new demands on the water supply and brought some new uses. One of the first big industries in the pioneer town was a brewery, which in later years had as its slogan, "It's the water that makes the difference."

Going back thousands of

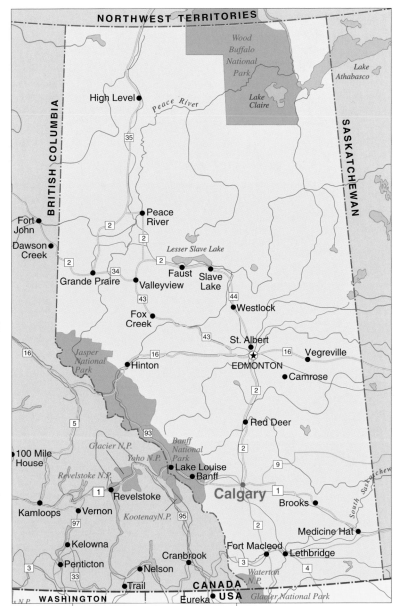

years in Calgary's history, water has always made the difference.

Geology

Calgary is built on geology. That's not unusual, of course, because geological processes are constantly at work all over

the world. In Calgary, however, those age-old processes have been closely studied, because geology is very important to the Calgary economy. Calgarians are famous for being forward-looking, but behind the popular image is another truth. Calgarians also

11

Transitions in Nature

NATURE HAS BEEN generous to Calgary.

Not only is the city just a short drive from the Rockies, one of the world's most spectacular mountain playgrounds, but within the city limits, a great variety of natural areas offer recreation.

The city is positioned at a dramatic transition point. To the east are the great plains. The big-sky, wheat-growing flatlands stretch out all the way to Winnipeg. To the west are the rolling foothills and the mountains.

It is within Calgary's city limits that those two dramatic landscapes—prairie and foothills—meet and come together to create a multitude of micro-ecological zones. The city parks department has surveyed the different natural environments around the rivers and hills of Calgary and has identified 10 general habitat types, ranging from wetlands and native grassland to aspen forest and white spruce forest. Even so-called "disturbed" lands that once were developed for agricultural or industrial purposes, but which are now being left alone, were studied and categorized. Each habitat type attracts an accompanying variety of wildlife.

Getting particular scrutiny were Calgary's major parks, especially Fish Creek Provincial Park in the south, the Weaslehead section of Glenmore Park in the west, Nose Hill Park in the north, and the riverbank areas along the Bow downstream from the Inglewood Bird Sanctuary.

The Bow and Elbow Rivers, as well as Fish Creek, provide natural avenues for wildlife to enter adjacent residential districts. It is not uncommon in some parts of the city for deer or even the occasional bear to venture near residential developments.

The greatest range of habitat types is at Fish Creek Provincial Park. The wetland regions along the creek are not large, but they form an important link with the

Dave Elphinstone, Naturalist

DAVE ELPHINSTONE is an author and naturalist for Calgary Parks and Recreation Department.

I think the key thing is seeing that nature isn't an extra—it's something that's integral to our lives. Having greenspace, and seeing green, really impacts on the quality of our life.

All you have to do is look at where there are ravines in a city; housing prices go up by $50,000 to $80,000 next to those ravines—and that tells you the value…I don't think that's esoteric; I think it's something much more ingrained. We've tried to separate ourselves as much from nature as we can, but we can't because we're part of it.

Just knowing something is there is important—knowing the bird sanctuary is there, or knowing Nose Hill is there—that's important. Even golf takes people into something they consider more natural. I wouldn't consider that more natural, but comparing an office building to golf, it is.

Birdwatching at one time was for people with pith helmets, but now just about everybody does it, if they ever look out their window and look at a house sparrow. But they would never consider themselves to be a birdwatcher. It's the same thing with environmental issues. A large number of people wouldn't consider themselves environmentalists, but what they do want to see is green shrubs out their window.

The difference is whether you call yourself one, or recognize that you're one. But the real issue is, "Do you partake in that enjoyment?" I'd say, in Calgary, there are probably very few people who don't.

Transitions in Nature

array of wetland sloughs sprinkled outside the city's southern boundaries. There are extensive fields of native grassland, as well as former agricultural and industrial lands that have been replanted and are now being rehabilitated. The spruce and poplar forest areas provide nesting sites for birds.

The largest wetlands region is in the Weaselhead area on the western edge of the Glenmore reservoir. The location has often been targeted for highway development, but environmental groups have repeatedly urged that it be preserved as a natural habitat.

When the creation of Nose Hill Park was first proposed, many hoped it would remain accessible to native wildlife. However, residential development has now encircled the parkland on all sides, making it an island of prairie nature in a sea of housing. The new development has made it all but impossible for wide-ranging animals such as coyotes and deer to ramble over the hill. Even so, there are still many other original animal residents, including porcupines, rabbits, and Richardson's ground squirrels (gophers).

Within Nose Hill Park, especially on the steep slopes around the brow of the hill, is one of the largest plots of undisturbed native fescue grassland yet remaining in North America. It hosts a wide variety of native wildflowers and flowering shrubs. Visitors are asked not to remove the flowers. Unfortunately, some parts of the grassland have become infested with weed species, especially

New environmental attitudes help preserve space for all living things, large and small

thistle; but various methods are being tested to remove the thistles without damaging the grasses.

The city's oldest nature preserve is the Inglewood Bird Sanctuary, which was established in 1929 by the family of pioneer Mountie Colonel James Walker. For many years, however, the land was owned by a major construction company, and gravel was mined on the site. It wasn't until 1970 that the sanctuary was taken over by the city parks department. Soon it became a centre of activity for all local environmental groups.

Each year the sanctuary is visited by almost 250 species of birds, from common house sparrows to rare bald eagles and turkey vultures. And each year, upwards of 50,000 birdwatchers and other nature-lovers come to see them.

Best Natural Areas

- Inglewood Bird Sanctuary
- Laycock Park
- Nose Hill Park
- Lowery Gardens
- Edworthy Park
- Bowmont Park
- Weaslehead Flats in Glenmore Park
- Carburn Park
- Fish Creek Park

know how to look back, literally millions of years. That's how they find oil.

Until around 60 million years ago, the Calgary region was a beach area on the western shore of a semi-tropical sea. The vegetation and sealife of the period was buried and became oil and gas. Sand deposited at the time is now the coarse-grained sandstone forming the bedrock beneath Calgary.

The sandstone, identified by geologists as the Paskapoo Formation, can be seen at outcrops along the cliffs surrounding the Glenmore Reservoir, on the slopes of Nose Hill, and along the cliffs above the Bow River on the city's western boundary.

Paskapoo sandstone has a beautiful, light brown colour and was used as a building material in Calgary until around 1920—by which time its faults were clear. The stone does tend to crumble if it is not kept dry, which is why it is only rarely used in construction projects now. However, large blocks of sandstone are still used for retaining walls and as decoration in public parks and private gardens.

Over the past two million years, geologists calculate, Calgary was buried by glaciers several times. The last ice age probably reached its maximum size between 15,000 and 18,000 years ago. At that time, Calgary was the meeting point between two major advancing

glaciers, one coming down from the mountains. An even larger body of ice spread west and south across the continent from the Hudson's Bay area. The glaciers churned up the land, thoroughly grinding and stirring rocks, sand and silt.

As the vast glaciers melted, a great lake called Glacial Lake Calgary formed. It is estimated the lake was more than 40 kilometres long and stretched up the Bow valley well beyond Cochrane. Geologists have identified several areas on both sides of the Bow valley showing clear evidence of once being the beaches of Lake Calgary.

The lake bottom, an area which now includes most neighborhoods in Calgary,

Squirrels

Native red squirrels have been displaced

SOME CALGARIANS LOVE them. Others hate them. They are the guests who came to stay—for keeps.

They are the grey and black squirrels who have taken up residence in Calgary's urban forest. They appear to be as natural here as prairie sunshine, but the truth is they are an introduced species that has displaced the native red squirrel.

Today there are thousands of them, ranging in color from deep black to light grey, living in every city district with enough tall trees to give them food and shelter.

In 1938, however, there were only seven. The seven were brought to Calgary from Ontario by Calgary's first zookeeper, Tom Baines. The squirrels were just another exotic exhibit at the zoo on St. George's Island, a nostalgic reminder for many Calgarians of what they had left behind in Eastern Canada.

The squirrels adjusted well to their new home. They moved out of the cages and into the trees on St. George's Island. Within a few

years, the zoo had more squirrels than it could handle.

As an experiment (one that zoo officials would never do today), six pairs were released along the well-treed riverbank of the Elbow River in the Elbow Park district. From there they began to spread across the city—and they've never stopped.

Now they make a merry sight as they scamper along fences and through tree branches. Some Calgarians love to feed them. A few squirrels even get so tame they will take food from the hand.

There are many gardeners, however, who get simply furious at what just one squirrel can do to a freshly-planted flowerbed. For them, the squirrel is nothing more than a saucy, four-legged, bushy-tailed weed!

rapidly filled with finer clay sediments.

Eventually the lake drained away, probably 10,000 to 12,000 years ago. But the Bow continued to flow, and it cut deeply into the old lake bottom. The result of the relatively rapid erosion can be seen in the dramatic cliffs and hillsides along the valley escarpments. Many of those hillsides and steep slopes are unstable and are often unsuitable for use as construction sites. City policy now states that the escarpment areas should be preserved as parkland.

The Bow River has changed its route over the centuries, wriggling its way along the bottom of the valley floor, and cutting into the hillsides. Geologists and archeologists have identified areas that once were channels of the river but now are many hundreds of metres

Centuries of glaciation helped create fertile prairie farmlands

from the riverbank. Many gardeners have done the same in their own backyards. Using only a simple shovel, they dug down and discovered, under the topsoil, there was nothing but gravel and water-smoothed stones.

Glacial Erratics

ONE OF THE MOST dramatic examples of the power of the glaciers once covering Calgary is the long necklace of large boulders that stretches along the foothills.

One of the rocks is a well-known landmark on the southern slopes of Nose Hill Park. The largest boulder is the Big Rock near Okotoks. Others like them can be found all the way from Edson to the Montana border.

The boulders are called *erratics* by geologists, a name reflecting their anomalous origin. They are made of a different kind of rock than everything else in the region. Together, the boulders are called the Foothills Erratics Train.

Geologists have traced the long string of erratic rocks to their source in the mountains near Jasper. They theorize that the boulders were scraped off a mountain by a glacier which then carried them south. When the ice melted, the boulders were left high and dry.

Later, as foothills and plains became grasslands, the boulders became important for the buffalo. The great shaggy beasts would rub and itch themselves on the rocks. Over the centuries, the constant rubbing by the buffalo has actually polished the sides of some of the erratic boulders. On ranches, herds of cattle continue the practice today.

Ice-scarred boulders dot foothills landscape

Spectacular Rocky Mountains are a popular recreational area for Calgarians and include a vast range of attractions, from gentle hiking trails to challenging climbing routes

The Canadian Rockies

The mountains are Calgary's big, psychic mascots.

When the sun is shining and the mountain tops are glistening with fresh-fallen snow, Calgarians all feel great. But when there's mist in the air, or if there are clouds on the horizon obscuring the peaks, folks in Calgary sense something isn't quite right.

They love the fabulous, jagged, western skyline. It doesn't matter that many of the mountains visible from Calgary are more than 100 kilometres away. It doesn't even matter that there are people in Banff and Canmore who actually live among the distant peaks. Calgarians still have an immense sense of ownership about the Rockies. Those are *our* mountains.

A house with a good view of the mountains will cost more than one that has a less-interesting view. Rents in many office towers are higher on those floors with windows facing the mountains.

For thousands of Calgarians, the mountain parks are prime weekend playgrounds. The parks act as magnets for anyone with a taste for natural adventure. Early Saturday morning there is a parade of fun-seekers headed to the mountains on the Trans-Canada Highway. Late Sunday evening the traffic flow on the highway reverses course as the campers, climbers, skiers, bikers, and hikers return home.

Exhilarating mountain vistas are just a short drive away

There seems to be no end to the variety of recreational opportunities, whether hiking or cycling along the trails in Kananaskis during the summer, or skiing at one of the many resort areas near Banff during the winter. There are even lakes for wind-surfing and scuba diving.

There are many prime viewpoints in Calgary for gazing at the mountains. One favorite is the top of the hill overlooking Stampede Park, and another is the top of Nose Hill. Until a few years ago, the Calgary Tower had the best view of all, but now there are too many new buildings in the way, obscuring the view.

Now the best viewing location is at the top of the ski jump tower at Canada Olympic Park. Regular tours are offered to the ski tower. As well, it is possible to rent the tower lounges for meetings and other private functions.

The best way to see the mountains, though, is to get right in them. There are several groups that organize bicycle tours on the picturesque highways during the summer months or offer back-country hikes on the mountain trails. In the winter, similar groups organize cross-country ski excursions over many of those very same trails.

As well, there are plenty of facilities for downhill skiing, with slopes suitable for everyone from rank beginners to ex-

Geology of the Rockies

IT'S HARD TO IMAGINE, but the Rockies once were flat. In fact, they were at the bottom of an ocean. They are made up of silts and sediments gathered on the ocean floor.

Slowly, the deposits were compressed and turned into rock by the weight of the water and sediments continuing to gather on the bottom. The process lasted for more than a billion years.

Then, about 120 million years ago, the sea bottom began to rise, the result of pressures created as the continental plate beneath North America collided with the plate beneath the sea.

The stresses buckled and folded the sedimentary rock strata, pushing the massive slabs of older rocks, hundreds of metres thick, on top of younger ones. As well, there were volcanoes spewing lava and ash atop the sedimentary layers.

The process created the Rockies and all the other mountain ranges along the western edge of the North American continent. The area around Calgary and Banff is relatively stable today. But as the eruption of Mount St. Helen's demonstrated, the mountain-building process is far from over.

perts. Just one hour out of the city is the Nakiska ski area which was used for downhill events during the 1988 Olympic Winter Games. Also close at hand is Fortress Mountain and the Canmore Nordic Centre.

The "big three" skiing developments within Banff National Park are Sunshine Village, Mystic Ridge/Norquay and Lake Louise.

Even so, many Calgarians rarely get to the mountains on a regular basis. They don't need to. After all, they see them every day. Those mountains are good, old friends.

Climate

"If you don't like the weather in Calgary, just wait five minutes and it'll change."

So goes an old joke about the unpredictability of Calgary's climate. The mountains get most of the blame, or credit, for the weather in

southern Alberta. The water-laden, air masses from the Pacific coast are driven up into high, cold altitudes by the Rockies, which drains them of moisture.

As a result, Calgary (like the rest of the foothills region) is in a "rain shadow" zone with low levels of precipitation throughout the year.

The low moisture content means the air in Calgary is generally sparkling clear. Mists and fogs are rare, although pollution, mostly from car ex-

hausts, can sometimes give the air above the city a dirty brown appearance.

The weather hardly ever follows the calendar. We can have hot, sunny days in January—warm enough to fool the trees into budding—and bitter, cold snow in September.

However, winters are usually mild, compared with other Canadian prairie cities, because of the frequent Chinook winds.

Summers are sweet and warm, and only rarely is the

Temperatures

CALGARY IS SOMETIMES called The Sunshine City because we get more hours of full sunlight than anywhere else in Canada. The average is 2,314.4 hours annually.

Other records:
• Days with measurable rain: 58
• Mean daily temperature

July/August: 22.7°C (72.9°F)
• Mean daily winter temperature: -8.9°C (16°F)
• Average duration of Chinook: 25 days
• Hottest day: July 25, 1933; 36.1°C (97°F)
• Coldest day: Feb. 4, 1893; -45°C (-49°F)

sun too hot for outdoor activities. The evenings bring a welcome cooling, and the twilight can last almost until midnight.

Winter blizzards do cause havoc, but even more dangerous are summer hailstorms. Calgary is on the fringe of Canada's "Hail Alley," a section of the province from Edmonton to Lethbridge that is battered by hail each summer.

The hailstorms are created by fluffy cumulus clouds building up over the foothills on hot, muggy, summer days. As the moisture in the clouds is lifted by updrafts into higher and colder elevations, it freezes and forms hailstones. Some reach the size of baseballs and grapefruit.

When a big hailstorm strikes a farm, the result can be a ruined crop, but when it hits a city like Calgary, it means millions of dollars of damage to roofs, cars, and

Chinook Tales

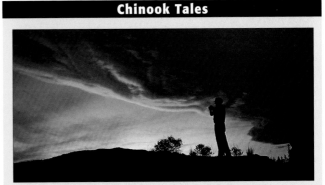

Famous Chinook Arch frames a glorious sunset

NATURALLY, THE CHINOOK has inspired a variety of jokes and legends, like the one about the pioneer postman. There was so much snow one winter that the town was buried in drifts, and he walked right over the houses.

He got to Cochrane when a Chinook struck; then he realized his mistake and had to swim back.

Or the folks who went for a sleigh ride. They were out in the country when the Chinook began.

They made a dash back to Calgary. The wind was blowing hard so they had to move quickly or they'd be caught in the field without snow. The horses were struggling in deep drifts, the front of the sleigh runners were riding in slush, and the back end was kicking up dust.

So the legends go.

For centuries, buffalo were monarchs of the plains

other property.

Chinook

The Chinook is Calgary's warm winter wind. The stiff, gusty breeze can pull the temperature out of the deep-freeze and send it rocketing into the springtime range.

Riding out a Chinook is an exhilarating experience. Every Calgarian has a story of stepping outdoors and expecting to feel the sting of winter on his or her cheeks but instead being greeted by the gentle warmth of the fair wind. Each winter, Calgarians will enjoy as many as 30 to 35 days of Chinooks.

These winds originate over the mountains and, like most of the breezes from that source, lose much of their moisture as they pass over the Rockies. When they hit Calgary, they are warm and dry; so snowdrifts shrink instantly when the breeze hits them.

The effect of the wind is instantaneous. Calgary's weather records include dozens of dramatic examples of the temperature climbing by as much as 25 degrees or

more in just an hour or two. One of the most extreme occurred in December of 1933.

On December 20 at 7 pm, the temperature was -16˚ C. Then the Chinook blew in,

Beaver

EVEN A FEW MINUTES spent watching a beaver at work will confirm the ancient adage. They really are, as the saying goes, busy as beavers.

Each year, they build dams and lodges along waterways in Calgary. If the beaver settles in a rustic wildlife park area along Nose Creek or Fish Creek, for instance, chances are it will not be disturbed.

Some years, beaver even build dams right downtown in the quiet channels at the downstream end of Prince's Island. There they do all the things they do in the wild—build lodges, cut down trees, munch on bark and

saplings, and raise their young, all under the eyes of curious office workers and other riverbank strollers.

However, sometimes the city parks department must prevent damage to trees whenever beavers build too near residential areas or in manicured parks. The first line of defence is simple. Light wire fencing is wrapped around vulnerable trees. If the wire isn't enough, or if a beaver dam causes the flood of low-lying areas and roadways, the animals are trapped and moved to more remote areas where they can't do any harm.

sending the thermometer to +3 by 8:30 and +6 by midnight. Around 2 am the Chinook stopped, and the cold returned; within an hour, the temperature was back to -15°

C.

The effect on people is even more dramatic. Children go outdoors in shirtsleeves to make snowballs. Automobiles, frozen solid for weeks, are

thawed and started. Icy sidewalks are cleared, and water flows in the streets.

Many gardeners fear the drying effect of the Chinook, which can kill garden plants by dehydrating exposed branches. One way to combat the wind is to wrap fragile plants, especially young ornamental trees and bushes, in burlap shrouds.

Falcons

IT'S A TOUGH WORLD, and getting tougher, for peregrine falcons.

Toxic pesticides have made it all but impossible for the birds to reproduce properly. And the natural habitats the birds prefer—high cliffs overlooking water—are disappearing.

Somehow, though, a few individuals of the endangered species have gone against nature and are nesting on Calgary office buildings.

The first pair appeared in 1982 on a ledge near the top of Alberta Government Telephones' Len Werry Building. Suddenly, office workers were treated to the dramatic sight of the peregrines catching (and killing) pigeons in mid-flight.

In nature, peregrines tend to nest on protected ledges high on cliffs

above rivers and streams. They are a migratory species and travel as far south as Mexico for the fall and winter.

The Werry Building, at the corner of 7th Avenue and 1st Street SW, houses long-distance telephone switching gear and is finished with grey, gravel-textured concrete. Some naturalists speculated the birds were attracted by the texture of the facing stone.

The original pair have since disappeared, but the theory garnered fresh support in the summer of 1994. A new pair nested on the nearby Scotia Centre tower, at the corner of the Stephen Avenue Mall (8th Avenue and 2nd Street SW), which also has grey, textured ledges.

Wherever the birds nest, they are kept under close scrutiny by the Wildlife Foundation and Alberta Parks Service. Any peregrine eggs which fail to hatch are replaced by chicks from the breeding facility at Wainwright.

Peregrines have suffered a severe decline in population because of the spread of toxic pesticides. Fortunately, the Wainwright program sends chicks to selected sites across the country in an attempt to re-establish the species.

Falcons nest on office towers

Animals

Animals have not completely given up on Calgary.

From time to time, it is possible to see a bald eagle flying over the rooftops of a residential district. A powerful beast of the air, the eagle appears to be about the size of a young black lab. To see one on the wing in the midst of the city is a holy moment.

And spectacular widewinged herons nest along the reedy banks of Nose Creek. They seem ungainly as they begin to fly, but when they gain speed, they are graceful and elegant. They are flying poems—like the birds depicted with just four, simple brush strokes by Japanese artists centuries ago.

Coyotes can be heard howling at the moon in some suburban districts near the city limits. They send chills up the spine and haunt the dreams.

But for all that, not much space has been left for the animals once living where Calgarians now have their bungalows, their townhouses, and apartments. Despite the enduring popularity of the old cowboy song, Calgary is no longer the sort of place,

Urbanization

Even Mount Royal was bald prairie in Calgary's early days

CALGARIANS HAVE transformed Calgary. It used to be prairie, and now it's a forest.

Once, the city was almost tree-less, except for a few areas along the riverbanks. Even in old neighborhoods like Mount Royal, which are now thick with trees, Calgary was originally bald prairie. Only a few knee-high wild rose bushes poked above the grass to challenge the horizon.

Almost every tree now thriving in Calgary was planted by hand. In fact, one of the best ways to judge the age of a neighborhood is to look at the trees planted there. It takes about a decade for the saplings to reach higher than the eavestrough on a suburban bungalow. And about half a century must pass before trees planted along both sides of a boulevard are big enough for their branches to form a canopy over the street as they do in Sunnyside and Hillhurst.

Creating this urban forest has been a significant alteration of the environment, a transformation as significant as the change from horse-drawn carriages to exhaust-spewing automobiles. Trees work hard to clean the air; their leaves remove dust and fumes, and release oxygen. They provide shade from the hot, prairie sun and provide nesting site for many species of birds—although not all birds are happy with trees. One of the casualties of the new forest is the western meadowlark. Its cheery call was once heard in all districts of the city, but in recent years, it has retreated to the outer fringes of the city in search of the open fields it prefers.

That there were few trees in Calgary was no accident. Before the settlers came, the native tribes used to burn off dead grass to encourage green growth the next spring for the buffalo. The grazing buffalo ate everything green, including young saplings.

Trees were important in the area's early history. Fort Calgary was built of logs from trees found upstream on the Elbow River. Logging became one of the city's first big industries. One sawmill operated by Peter Prince was set up on an island in the Bow River. Ever since then, the island has been called Prince's Island. It is now one of the city's most popular parks.

Pioneer entrepreneur William Pearce was the first Calgarian to promote the value of trees. He brought thousands of young seedlings from the mountains to Calgary. Today, it is estimated that almost two million trees are thriving in the city. Some of the best-loved are the poplars along Memorial Drive, which were planted to honor soldiers who died in the First World War.

The oldest trees in Calgary are found in a grove of Douglas firs on the north bank of the Bow just below the Spruce Cliff district. Some of the firs are between 400 and 450 years old, making them the oldest living creatures in the city. They were the size of Christmas trees when William Shakespeare was a lad on his way to school. A sturdy staircase trail has been built through the grove. Visitors are asked to stay on the trail to protect the sensitive roots of the firs from being trampled.

"where the buffalo roam, and the deer and the antelope play."

The buffalo once was undisputed king of the prairies. Before the settlers came, there were herds of buffalo the size of seas. Explorers and fur-traders have left accounts of seeing herds that stretched from one side of the horizon to the other. Herds on the move would take three or four days to pass.

Then the extermination began in earnest as the industrial society of North America moved west. The herds disappeared from the Calgary area by 1880, and the species was brought to the very brink of extinction by 1885.

Conservation measures revived the herds in the 20th century, but by then the prairies were settled by farmers and ranchers. The buffalo was imprisoned in national parks.

The deer, elk, and antelope were hunted down, too. Now they survive only in parks or in remote rural areas. Also long gone are the brown bear and the great prairie grizzly which once roamed over the Calgary hills.

About the only animal species to survive city life are small and inoffensive. Wild rabbits and hares sometimes run—or stand stalk-still—in city parks or on city streets near the rivers. There are still colonies of the common gopher, the Richardson's Ground Squirrel, in all corners of the city. A large group even nested in burrows dug into the hillside at the top end of the Centre Street Bridge—that is until a city crew of pest control

Fishing

THE BOW IS A fisherman's dream stream and so is the Elbow.

Anglers elsewhere have to travel for hours to find a favorite fishing hole, but in Calgary fishermen can simply stop by the riverbank on their way home after work.

They grab their gear out of the trunk or the back of the pickup and cast their lines.

Some fish from the many bridges across the rivers. Others prefer to seek out shady, quiet backwaters. One of the most popular places is the slowly-spinning whirlpool on the Bow just a few hundred metres upstream from Crowchild Bridge. Another favorite is along the north bank of the Bow opposite Fort Calgary Park. Many of the rainbow trout end up as dinner, but more and more sportsmen are adopting the catch-and-release philosophy, especially with the rarer species, the brown trout.

Bow bait

officers got rid of them.

Nature Gardens

Gardeners have a rough row to hoe in Calgary.

It takes a brave heart to stir the foothills soil in the springtime. Unlike other areas of the world, where gorgeous and flamboyant plants leap out of the ground of their own volition, in Calgary, flowers and greenery grow slowly.

The climate can be cruel. The gardener is hostage to the elements. Late frosts in spring freeze the first green shoots. Hot summer winds shrivel the

Trees

THERE'S ONLY ONE way to accurately gauge the age of a tree. That's to count the growth rings.

In the old days, scientists would estimate the age of a grove of trees by choosing one or two representative trees and then cutting them down! The only method of getting at the growth rings, to tell how long a tree had lived, was to kill it.

Fortunately, a better method has been devised. To estimate the age of the Douglas firs along the north bank of the Bow River, researchers use a special drill to extract an interior core about the size of a spaghetti noodle. The rings are counted in the lab, and the tiny hole left by the coring machine is plugged with a sterile glue to prevent further damage.

Calgary abounds with recreational areas where everyone can get close to nature

tender leaves. Hail pounds the fruit from the tree and beats the blossoms to the ground.

Even worse, an early autumn snowfall ends the season far too soon. The gardener says goodnight to a spectacular display of fragrant blooms and awakes to see ice-covered stalks standing naked and forlorn in the flowerbeds.

And yet, year after year, Calgary gardeners persist. Against all the odds that capricious nature can stack against them, they succeed in creating their own versions of paradise.

William Pearce

In pioneer days, gardeners began the struggle to transform the stark grassland into parks and gardens almost as soon they got a roof over their heads.

One of the most influential pioneer leaders was William Pearce, the Canadian Pacific Railway land agent. He could gaze at Calgary's barren hills

and valleys and imagine them covered with trees. There were no "garden centres" then, so to put his dream into action, he sent work parties to the mountains. They came back with boxcars loaded with young pine, spruce, and fir. The trees were sold to Calgarians for five cents apiece.

Pearce's voice was persuasive. In 1885, he convinced Ottawa to donate the land for Central Park (now Central Memorial Park). Then the park, on 11th Avenue between 3rd and 4th Streets SW, was the edge of the town. The area was landscaped, and although some details of the planting have changed or matured over the decades, the basic lay-out remains. The park is still Calgary's finest formal public garden.

Before the landscaping was complete, however, the land was used as a temporary tree farm for the young trees from

the mountains. As well, maple trees were brought from Brandon, Manitoba.

The CPR, itself, set an early example. In 1891, an ornamental garden was built next to the station and remained there until the site was taken over a dozen years later to build the Palliser Hotel.

As early as 1895—again largely at the urging of Pearce—tree planting began along one of the city's main arteries, Atlantic Avenue (now 9th Avenue). About 80 trees were planted at a cost to the citizens of $12. Some of the trees were damaged, so in 1899, a bylaw was passed to protect the trees from vandalism.

Pearce's drive and determination have proven an inspiring example to later generations. The streetside tree-planting program had been allowed to lapse, but in the mid-1970s, in time for the centennial of the founding of Fort Calgary, trees were planted throughout the downtown core and adjacent neighborhoods.

William Reader

The most important gardening activist after Pearce was William Reader, who came to Calgary from England in 1908. He was a founder of the Calgary Horticultural Society and became the city's Park Superintendent in 1913.

Despite tight budgets imposed by council throughout the 1920s and the Dirty '30s, Reader applied the principles of the then-popular City Beautiful movement.

He designed, or modified, all city parks and cemeteries until his retirement in 1942. He died only a few weeks later in 1943. At the instigation of the Calgary Horticultural Society, city council named the extensive rock garden at the northern end of Union Cemetery in his honor.

Since then, unfortunately, the Reader Rock Garden has not been maintained as well as when Reader, himself, was able to give it his personal attention.

Vacant Lots

Early Calgarians weren't the sort to let the wild grass grow under their feet—not even in the vacant lots which once made up a sizable portion of the city. Their solution was the Vacant Lots Garden Club.

The problem arose because the rocketing growth that marked the first decade of the century came to a sudden stall in 1911. By then, real estate developers had plotted out subdivisions for kilometres in every direction. Trouble was, many of the lots surveyed went unsold, and many others reverted to the city because their purchasers were unable to build or even pay the taxes.

The Vacant Lots Garden Club was organized in 1914 to put the idle land to use. The prairie sod was ploughed, and vegetables and flowers were planted in hundreds of lots all around the city. Potatoes were judged to be the best for breaking in a new plot, so seed potatoes were sold at cost to members of the club.

The organization continued until after the Second World War when the influx of newcomers needing homes sparked a building boom and put an end to the surplus of vacant lots.

The wild rose is Alberta's floral emblem

Xeric Garden

CALGARY HAS A DRY climate and water resources are limited, so many gardeners are turning to *xeric* gardening.

Xeric, (Greek for *dry*), gardening stresses the use of hardy plants that do not require extensive watering, and the creation of other sorts of ground cover instead of the traditional thirsty lawn.

To reduce water wastage through evaporation, watering should be done in the early morning. Organic mulches such as bark chips and compost help retain moisture and add nutrients.

Appropriate plants for Calgary include:

Annuals: marigolds, zinnias, cornflowers, morning glory, dusty miller, African daisy, and sweet alyssum.

Perennials: moss phlox, hens and chicks, sedum, Iceland poppy, snow in summer, and bearded iris.

Trees/Shrubs: caragana, Nanking cherry, Colorado spruce, potentilla, honeysuckle, and common lilac.

3. Highlights of History

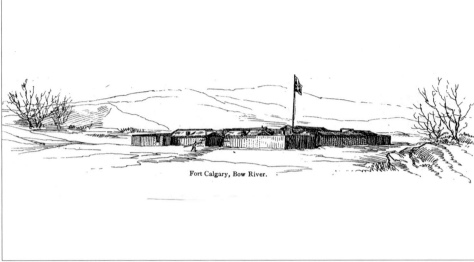

Fort Calgary, Bow River.

The members of Troop F of the North West Mounted Police chose a picturesque location for Fort Calgary

Written history about Calgary goes back only a century or so, but the unwritten part is much older. Almost every schoolkid, for instance, knows that the city once had a climate like Jamaica and was inhabited by dinosaurs. It's too bad there was nobody around to enjoy the climate then, because those were important days for Calgary 60 to 400 million years ago. Plants and marine animals were buried and slowly were turned into coal and oil and gas. They became the fuel that keeps Calgary's economy ticking today.

Much later, about fifteen thousand years ago, the area was buried by ice when glaciers swept over the continent. As the ice age ended, Calgary went to the bottom of Lake Calgary.

Archeological evidence indicates Calgary's first human residents turned up not long after the lake drained away, about 10,000 to 12,000 years ago. They began to enjoy the good life, exploiting the natural resources, especially the buffalo.

6300 BC – Hunters slay bison in southwest Calgary near 17th Avenue shopping district. Later, similar hunting party, there in 3300 BC drop weapons and tools imported from Montana. Hunt location is now occupied by Mount Royal Village and still a great place to go hunting—for up-scale bargains, not buffalo.

1787 – Hudson's Bay Company trader David Thompson visits native peoples near Calgary. He is believed to be first European to see region.

1870 – Federal government purchases Northwest Territories, including the prairie provinces, from Hudson's Bay Company.

1871 – Spitzee whiskey fort built by Montana traders on Highwood River south of Calgary.

1873 – North West Mounted Police created to combat whiskey trade and affirm Canada's claim on western plains.

1875 – Fort established by NWMP where Bow and Elbow rivers meet. Inspector Ephrem Brisebois names fort after himself.

1876 – NWMP Colonel Macleod urges new name for Fort Brisebois, suggests calling it Calgary.

1877 – Treaty No. 7 signed at Blackfoot Crossing near Cluny by leaders of all native tribes in southern Alberta.

1879 – Native hunters alarmed by sudden scarcity of buffalo.

1880 – Buffalo herds are gone. Sarcee tribe (now the Tsuu T'Ina Nation) faces starvation and threatens to burn Fort Calgary unless food is provided. Confrontation ends peacefully when tribe agrees to go to Fort Macleod for food rations.

1881 – Marquis of Lorne, the Governor General of Canada, tours prairies. Names Alberta after his wife, the Princess Louise Caroline Alberta, fourth daughter of Queen Victoria.

1883 – CPR arrives in Calgary on August 11, providing village with direct link to the rest of Canada and the world. *Calgary Herald* begins publication. Railway spurns pioneer settlement on east side of Elbow River and builds station on bald prairie west of town; chagrined townsfolk follow railway's lead and cross the river, where they must buy land from CPR land company.

1884 – Baker F. J. Claxton builds first frame building on new townsite for his Star Bakery. Village gets charter to become town.

1885 – Northwest Rebellion, led by Louis Riel, sends shivers through nervous Calgarians, but local tribes remain peaceful.

1886 – The Great Fire reduces 14 buildings to ashes and prompts citizens to upgrade fire department. Afterwards, many new buildings are made of local sandstone, giving Calgary short-lived nickname, "The Sandstone City."

1892 – CPR builds branch line to Edmonton, making Calgary key distribution point for settlers.

1894 – Town receives charter to become first city in Northwest Territories.

What's in a Name?

"CLEAR RUNNING WATER" is what Colonel James F. Macleod thought *Calgary* meant in Gaelic—or so he told his superiors in the North West Mounted Police in 1876. He was wrong, however, and his error continues to be cited as fact more than a century later.

Macleod suggested "Calgary" as a name for the Mountie fort, built in the fall of 1875, where the sprightly Elbow River flows into the mighty Bow. He thought it was more appropriate than the original name, Fort Brisebois, which the first commanding officer, Inspector Ephrem Brisebois, had proposed.

Macleod was right. After all, "Calgary" is much easier on the ear than "Brisebois," but he was completely wrong about its meaning. "Clear running water" in Gaelic is *t-shruthain shoilleir*.

Scholars had long been troubled by Macleod's explanation,

Colonel Macleod

but not until the 1975 centennial of the city's founding did one of Canada's foremost historians, Dr. George F.G. Stanley, set the record straight.

Dr. Stanley knew it must have been Calgary Bay in Scotland, a remote cove on the Isle of Mull, that Macleod was thinking of when he came up with the name. The hills enclosing the Scottish cove are rounded and treeless, and even now look very much like the hills surrounding the Mountie fort.

Stanley found that Calgary Bay has a long history in Scotland, and the name turns up in various forms in historical archives. Records show, in 1675, it was spelled *Calligourie*. It was usually *Calagaraidh* until the early 1800s, when the current spelling was adopted.

Despite the variations, though, the name always had the same meaning according to the Gaelic experts Stanley consulted. The *calli* or *cala* part means bay or cove. And the *gourie* or *garaidh* means farm or garden. So Calgary really means Bay Farm—or, to put it more poetically, Cove Garden.

1904 – Bob Edwards moves his *Eye Opener* newspaper to Calgary; soon it will be the most popular paper in Western Canada.

1905 – Alberta becomes a province, although Ottawa retains control over resources. Calgarians offended because Edmonton is capital.

1909 – Calgary Municipal Railway begins service.

1911 – City hall opens.

1912 – Calgary public library completed with $50,000 grant from US industrialist Andrew Carnegie. First Stampede held.

1913 – Boxer Luther McCarty dies in a Calgary arena in first round of fight with Arthur Pelkey for heavyweight championship of the world. City council hires renowned landscape architect and urban planner Thomas Mawson to advise on city's growth; his suggestions are shelved as building boom fizzles.

1914 – Oil discovered at Turner Valley; Calgary is centre of oil stock speculation.

1914-18 – First World War hits Calgary hard as thousands of young men enlist to defend the British Empire; hundreds do not return.

1915 – Centre Street Bridge opens.

1919 – Prince of Wales visits Calgary and falls in love with the wild west. He purchases EP ranch south of city. Second Stampede held.

1921 – Hillhurst (Louise) Bridge opens.

1922 – Radio stations CFAC and CFCN (now Mix 1060) both begin broadcasting. Calgary's Hillhurst soccer team wins national championship even though two players suffer broken legs in final game.

1923 – Stampede officially named part of the Calgary Exhibition and becomes annual attraction.

1930 – Calgary lawyer R. B. Bennett becomes prime minister of Canada for five frustrating years during depths of economic depression.

1935 – Social Credit, a new party with unorthodox economic views, wins provincial election; Calgary schoolteacher William Aberhart becomes premier.

1939 – King George VI visits city briefly. He is first reigning monarch to set foot on Calgary soil.

1939-45 – The Second World War brings an end to Depression. The strong demand for oil drains Turner Valley oilfield south of Calgary.

1947 – Oil well Leduc No.1 comes in, consolidating Calgary's position as head office for most Canadian oil companies.

1948 – Calgary's football team, the Stampeders, wins Grey Cup. First parking meters installed downtown.

1950 – City streetcars make last run as buses take over transit chores.

1951 – Princess Elizabeth and husband Prince Philip visit Calgary; Stampede holds special rodeo in chilly October weather for royal couple.

1954 – Oilman Eric Harvie establishes Glenbow Foundation

Marilyn Monroe

to handle his historical collections.

1955 – Alberta celebrates 50th year of as province. Calgary selected for Operation Lifesaver, Canada's largest-ever civil defence exercise; most Calgarians ignore mock air-raid sirens.

1956 – Mayor Don Mackay "borrows" 35 bags of cement from city department to build basement for holiday home in Banff. He later replaces cement but damage to reputation is irreversible.

1957 – Jubilee Auditorium opens.

1959 – Judicial inquiry finds Mayor Mackay used improper advantage to get cement and other benefits; voters oust him at fall election.

1960 – University of Alberta (Calgary) opens campus in city's northwest.

1964 – Heritage Park opens.

1967 – Centennial of Confederation; Calgarians celebrate by building planetarium and creating Confederation Park. University gains autonomy from U of A and becomes University of Calgary.

1972 – Stampeders win Grey Cup for second time.

1973 – Oil prices begin to skyrocket, launching city on frenzy of high-riding growth. Struggle begins between Ottawa and province over oil revenues; federal intervention prompts rude bumper sticker telling the East it could freeze in the dark.

1975 – Deerfoot Trail opens. City celebrates centennial; frustrated country singer Cal Cavendish marks event with low-level flight, circling Calgary Tower and bombing city streets with 100 records and 100 pounds of pig manure; no one is hurt, but Cavendish's pilot license is revoked.

1976 – Downtown becomes one large construction site as building boom transforms skyline.

1979 – Joe Clark, a sometime Calgarian, becomes prime minister but loses office in less than one year.

1980 – New Liberal government invokes National Energy Policy on October 28 and cripples thriving oil industry; within weeks, dozens of construction projects are left unfinished. Radio newsman Ralph Klein is elected mayor. Flames hockey team moves from Atlanta to Calgary, putting city in National Hockey League.

1981 – Oil prices slump. City wins bid to host '88 Winter Olympic Games. C-Train commences operation.

1983 – First food bank opens as recession hits city hard.

1988 – Winter Olympics light up a city struggling with a sluggish economy.

1992 – Stampeder fans celebrate third Grey Cup victory. Ex-mayor Ralph Klein becomes premier of Alberta.

1993 – Reform Party led by Calgarian Preston Manning transforms political map of Canada in federal election, taking almost all seats in Western Canada.

1994 – Calgary celebrates centennial of city.

1995 – Historic Louise Bridge restored to former glory with reinforced concrete arches topped off with authentic reproductions of original, ornate handrails and lampposts.

Prince of Wales

Calgarians were thrilled when Prince bought ranch in foothills

CALGARIANS FELL IN love with the Prince of Wales when he visited the city in 1919. The handsome bachelor had more charisma than a rock star. He bought a ranch in the foothills but visited it rarely, even after 1936 when he abdicated as King Edward VIII and retired in exile as the Duke of Windsor.

Politics

CALGARY IS A *VERY* political city. Two Calgarians have become prime minister, and many of the province's most powerful premiers have come from Calgary. In fact, on three occasions political protest parties have been launched from Calgary.

The remarkable achievement is unmatched by any other Canadian city.

It was in Calgary that the Social Credit party was formed during the Depression of the 1930s. Although the party was never able to implement most of its unusual economic theories, it ruled Alberta from 1935 until 1971. In slightly different form, Social Credit also dominated politics in British Columbia from 1952 until the late 1980s.

Social Credit was essentially a right-wing party, but Calgary also was the launching pad for Canada's most prominent party on the left. A convention in July 1932 began the Co-operative Commonwealth Federation. Despite its ungainly name, the CCF went on to form the government in Saskatchewan in 1944, becoming the first Socialist government in North America.

Later re-named the New Democratic Party, it would form governments in every province between BC and Ontario—every province, that is, except its birthplace Alberta.

The latest party to be launched from Calgary is the Reform Party of Canada, led by Preston Manning, which made political history in 1993 when it came within two seats of becoming the Official Opposition.

As well, some of Alberta's most powerful and influential premiers have come from Calgary.

Calgary lawyer John Brownlee, premier from 1925 to 1934, fought Ottawa for control of Alberta's resource industries. Until he won the case in 1929, Alberta had been, in effect, a second-class province because Ottawa had retained resource powers when the province entered Confederation in 1905.

Unfortunately, Brownlee is best remembered today for a sexual scandal. He had an affair with his young secretary, the details of which made torrid reading in Depression-era newspapers and led to the downfall of his government.

Brownlee's party was tossed out of office by Social Credit, led by a Calgary teacher, William Aberhart, the principal of Crescent Heights High School. Aberhart had used a radio program about Social Credit economic theories to build support across the province. The federal government, however, prevented Aberhart from implementing the most radical elements of Social Credit philosophy.

When Aberhart died in 1943, he was succeeded by his right-hand man, Ernest Manning, a former Saskatchewan resident who had been drawn to Calgary by Aberhart's Social Credit gospel.

Manning ruled a quarter-century, stepping down in 1968. He then became a senator and quietly cheered the political ambitions of his son, Preston.

Social Credit failed to survive the transition when Manning left. It lost to the Progressive Conservative Party, which had been revived by Peter Lougheed, a lawyer from—where else?—Calgary.

Lougheed, like Brownlee, had to fight Ottawa for control of Alberta's natural resources. He lost a crucial round when the federal Liberals brought in the National Energy Policy (NEP) in 1980.

Today, yet another Calgarian is premier. Ralph Klein, a plain-speaking, former radio newsman who had been Calgary's mayor throughout the turbulent 1980s, is leading Alberta through a profound re-structuring of government and society.

Calgary's two prime ministers, R.B. Bennett and Joe Clark, were both Tories and both had a frustrating time in office.

Robert Bedford Bennett was born in New Brunswick in 1870. He came to Calgary in 1893 and became a prominent social leader in pioneer Calgary. He was one of the most powerful lawyers in Alberta. Among his clients was the Canadian Pacific Railway, which then had influence second only to the government.

Bennett became leader of the Conservatives in 1927 and led his party to victory in 1930. Unfortunately, he was unable to deal with the problems caused by the Depression and became the scornful butt of popular humor. For instance, broken-down cars pulled by horses were called "Bennett buggies." The humor reflected the political will of the people, and Bennett lost the 1935 election to the Liberals, led by Mackenzie King.

When R.B. retired from public life, he was honored with a

Politics

R. B. Bennett (with cane) was the first Calgarian to become prime minister of Canada

British title, becoming Viscount Bennett. He moved to England and died there in 1947.

Charles Joseph (Joe) Clark was born in 1939 south of Calgary in High River, where his father ran the local paper. Joe was a cub reporter at the *Calgary Herald* in the late 1950s. Later, Clark moved to Edmonton and Ottawa, but often he returned to Calgary and for a time worked at *The Albertan* newspaper, writing headlines and editing stories.

He became leader of the PC party in 1976 and became prime minister in May of 1979. At 39, he was the youngest prime minister in Canadian history and the first born in Western Canada. However, his minority government lost a crucial vote of non-confidence in December and the Liberals regained office in February 1980.

Clark lost the leadership of his party in 1983 but served as a senior cabinet minister under Prime Minister Brian Mulroney. In 1994 he returned to Calgary where he now is a consultant on international trade.

4. Life in the City

Calgarians are proud of Western traditions

Maybe Calgary could have been an ordinary city like Edmonton or Winnipeg. It could have been as boring as Ottawa or as smug as Toronto the Good. But something happened. And that something was the first Stampede. It showed pioneer Calgarians that theirs

was a special city. The Stampede taught Calgarians there were some ideals to live up to concerning western hospitality.

The first Stampede blew into Calgary like a wild west wind in September of 1912. The rodeo was supposed to be an alternative to the annual agricultural exhibition and flower show. It was a one-time show-biz spectacular, a final farewell salute to the dying way of life on the open range.

The Stampede's sponsors were four wealthy Calgarians who became known forever after as the Big Four: George Lane, Pat Burns, Archie McLean and A.E. Cross. They were coaxed into it by Guy Weadick, an ambitious, touring showman who had performed in Calgary a few years earlier.

Weadick and the Big Four were building on a grand tradition of wild west shows which

dated all the way back to Buffalo Bill Cody's traveling extravaganzas.

Weadick himself was a veteran trick rider and his wife, whose show name was Flora La Due, was a lariat artist.

Wild west shows were very popular then. Old Buffalo Bill, with his flowing white hair and his hoopla, his fancy riders and his trick-shot artists, had even performed for Queen Victoria in England; his show was a hit across Europe.

But in Calgary in 1912, the "wild west" wasn't something rare and exotic that came from afar. There was plenty of it close at hand; and more importantly, it wasn't ever going to go away. The key elements—horses, cowboys, and the native people—had roots so deep that they would never disappear.

It's so easy to get into the Stampede spirit. In fact, it's hard not to feel that spirit.

It is possible to create a separate wardrobe for high-fashion stampeding—fancy boots, cowboy shirt, elegant neck scarf, pants or skirt, all topped off with a genuine cowboy hat.

Getting the right hat could

be the most difficult decision of all. Some like their hats to be spotless. Others prefer hats that look like they've been worn in the hot sun, pelted by the driving rain, and scuffed in the dust. For the perfectionist, getting it right can take several weeks.

But many Calgarians take a simpler (and cheaper) approach. They just wear a comfy pair of blue jeans.

Jeans are enough, almost. All jeans need to look authentic is a wide leather belt with a big, shiny belt buckle. Then add just one more item—shirt, boots, hat—and you're there: Instant Cowperson.

That's the great beauty of the Stampede. It really doesn't take much (or cost much) to

join in the fun.

And fun is what it's all about.

Normally staid corporations get into the swing of things by encouraging office workers to ignore the regular dress code. At many companies, workers are given the morning off on Parade Day so they can watch.

City council adjourns for the duration. No business meetings are held; instead the mayor and aldermen are kept busy with a vast round of informal Stampede functions.

Most stores take full advantage of the western theme. They decorate their windows and retail displays with bales of hay, wagon wheels, and other rustic artifacts. Service

BBQ

THE PREMIER SOCIAL events of Stampede are the Stampede Breakfast and the Stampede Barbecue. They are pure expressions of Stampede spirit, especially the breakfast.

Dozens of free Stampede Breakfasts are held around the city each year. The classic one is cooked on a portable stove at the back end of an old chuckwagon. At some of the larger breakfasts, there's simply not enough room for a wagon, so the cooking is done on portable industrial stoves.

The food is simple. Flapjacks are cooked on a griddle and served with bacon or sausages. Usually there's a large pot of beans, too, for those who can handle beans so early in the day.

Major corporations vie with one another to attract breakfast guests, or they simply provide a breakfast for their employees.

Naturally, at company ones, the bosses have to pull on aprons and serve the employees. That's the true Stampede style.

The Stampede Barbecue comes later in the day—and generally the beverages served are much stronger than coffee or tea. Some feature nothing fancier than hot dogs or hamburgers, but the best have great slabs of prime Alberta beef.

The menu depends on who's sponsoring the particular Stampede Barbecue. Anyone can do it; and thousands do, even if they're just inviting a few friends over on a warm Stampede evening.

But the Stampede Barbecue can be much more than an informal meal. In recent years it has tak-

en on a life of its own and has become a political institution of prime importance. No politician at any level—civic, provincial and federal — can afford to ignore the barbecue tradition. Warring political parties even boast publicly about how many guests came to their barbecue. The one with the most is almost guaranteed to win the next election.

Pickup trucks are practical and popular

stations and supermarkets have their windows painted with comic pictures of cowboys getting bucked off high-kicking horses.

The streets are fancied up a few weeks in advance. Brightly-colored banners are attached to lampposts along major thoroughfares and to traffic light standards at major intersections.

All the fuss and fancy stuff pay off. The Stampede puts a shine on Calgary that lasts all year round.

Wheels

Calgary is a city on the move. Mobility has always been the key to happiness here. Part of the reason is that destinations on the western plains are often far apart. The phenomenon has been well studied by scholars, such as Wallace Steg-

ner, who have found that the westerner's need for quick and easy transportation can be traced back to the days of the horse.

Cars have been part of the community's way of life since the first gas-guzzlers arrived in 1904. Today, the city is absolutely "car-friendly." Bike-riders and pedestrians have to take the back seat because there's no doubt when a Calgary motorist is behind the wheel.

It's true that many improvements for cyclists, walkers, and runners have been made in recent years. An extensive network of pathways and protected routes has been laid out to keep muscle-power advocates at a safe distance from gas-powered vehicles. But the big money in the transportation budget still goes to take care of the automobile.

The results include some of

John Gilchrist

THE DEAN OF *Calgary's restaurant critics is John Gilchrist. His reviews have been entertaining morning listeners on CBC Radio's* The Calgary Eye Opener *for 15 years.*

What I think is great about dining in Calgary is the incredible breadth. We have so many different kinds of cuisine here—not necessarily a lot of depth—and surprisingly good quality and good prices.

Calgarians tend to travel a lot and I think there's a real affinity with Asian food here. Much of the oil business takes people into Asia, and there are a lot of very high-quality Asian restaurants here. I think that's our strength.

There's also a north-south affinity, and we see the whole California style of cuisine that has come up through Seattle and Vancouver has spilled over into Calgary. You see that much more strongly than you do in eastern cities.

I would rate Calgary the third-best city in Canada for dining, following Montreal and Vancouver. Certainly we benefit from our international scope. You can go into cities our size in Europe and not find very much at all compared to what we have here. I think we have a pretty sophisticated dining clientele, with high demands. They're fickle, they hop from the latest trend to latest trend, but generally we can be pretty happy with what we've got here. I go to larger cities in the US and Europe and come back thinking we're not so hard done by.

the most impressive examples of transportation engineering in Western Canada. Calgary drivers are pampered with spacious interchanges, elegant bridges and overpasses, and gently curving high-speed roadways. Almost all of them have been artfully set into the landscape in a way that minimizes environmental damage. In fact, many have been built in a fashion that enhances the beauty of the land.

Driving along Calgary's main thoroughfares is a visual treat. Many of the roadways present stunning vistas and viewpoints. Since Calgarians spend so much time in their cars, dressing up the roadways is an appropriate way to create a modern City Beautiful. For instance, there's a point along Memorial Drive, just west of Crowchild Trail a few dozen metres before Memorial becomes Parkdale Boulevard, where the westbound motorist is presented with a spectacular view up the Bow River.

The city roadways abound with similar viewpoints. Motorists coming into the downtown core along Elbow Drive are presented with a grand glimpse of the skyline at the brow of the Britannia hill. Even more dramatic is the sudden sight of the distant downtown offered to southbound drivers cruising along 14th Street by Nose Hill Park in the city's northwest.

All along the rim of the hills encircling the downtown, there are similar vistas: along Sarcee Trail southbound beneath Broadcast Hill, along Memorial Drive westbound

Calgary mountaineers thrive on challenges

from the eastern edge of the city, on Centre Street descending from Crescent Heights. And the sight of the downtown skyline from the top of the new Langevin Bridge is an image that deserves to be put in a movie.

The city parks department

Laurie Skreslet, Mountaineer

LAURIE SKRESLET, the first Canadian to climb Mount Everest, sees mountains as a place of spiritual rejuvenation.

Calgary is a very unique place. I think you really need to be an outdoor person to bring out the best that this city can give you.

Mountains can change people—that's what they do—from a metaphysical or physical sense. They create change. One of the native people, many years ago, said to me, "The land speaks, but you have to learn first the language."

And he said, "You're learning it, and you don't know it just yet. In time it's going to come. You'll hear the land talk to you, and the land can tell you what's going to happen."

Over the years I got frustrated. I'd sit there and I couldn't hear a damn thing. It was when I gave up that the change started to happen—and I hear it, and I see it. I see it all the time. That magic is so strong in this province—and it's one of the reasons I think Calgary is such a great place to live.

Trail Names

STREETS IN CALGARY do more than carry traffic. Many of the city's thoroughfares carry a burden of history, and they do it in unique Calgary style.

Elsewhere in the world, a trail is little more than a narrow path winding its way through a wilderness area. In Calgary, however, the designation is reserved for some of the city's major roadways. It's one of Calgary's most obvious ways of promoting its wild west heritage.

The city's busiest north-south freeway is Deerfoot Trail. It has direct connections with many, major industrial arteries, including Blackfoot Trail and Peigan Trail.

Macleod Trail is one of the city's oldest roads and is still one of the major routes southward to Fort Macleod. Edmonton Trail is now a secondary route, but it once was the city's most important one north.

Crowchild Trail and Sarcee Trail are major thoroughfares in the city's southwest, and Stoney Trail is the name proposed for a planned route in the northwest. Bow Trail leads motorists westward out of the downtown core alongside the Bow River.

Many of the names reflect Calgary's historical ties with native people. The Blackfoot tribe now calls itself the Siksika Nation, and the Sarcee tribe is now the Tsuu T'Ina Nation, but the old names are still honored on Calgary street signs.

The Crowchild, a major north-south route in the city's west side, bears the name of the late David Crowchild, a highly-respected elder from the Tsuu T'Ina Nation.

The most colorful name, appropriately, is on the longest and fastest freeway, the Deerfoot Trail. The Deerfoot was named after a fleet-footed runner from the Siksika Nation named Api-kai-ees.

Api-kai-ees's name loses much of its charm when translated into English. Literally, it means "Scabby Dried Meat." Small wonder, then, that pioneer gamblers gave Api-kai-ees a more agreeable nickname, Deerfoot, when he took part in local foot races in the 1880s.

Deerfoot was as much a showman as a runner. He once gave an opponent a six-lap lead and still came in the winner. He was a long, lean man almost two metres tall and had considerable charisma. He was acknowledged as the leader of the small Siksika encampment that existed in those days near where Nose Creek joins the Bow, not far from where Memorial Drive intersects with Deerfoot Trail.

Unfortunately, Deerfoot often got into trouble with alcohol and with the law. He died of tuberculosis in a Calgary jail cell in 1897 and was buried in an unmarked grave.

has worked hard to embellish major roadway projects with attractive plantings. Colorful shrubs have been planted on steep cutbanks. Special care has been taken to form natural-looking groves of evergreen spruce trees on slopes along major freeways.

The plantings not only seem to soften the edges of the hard concrete overpasses, by providing visual variety, they also help reduce road noise for residents—and they help filter dust and exhaust fumes. They also provide strategic hiding places for police officers with radar or with the Multanova camera, which automatically takes a photograph of the licence plate of all cars traveling above the speed limit.

Of course, not every Calgary driver fully appreciates the value of the roadway system. All it takes is one minor traffic jam, one unfilled pothole, or poorly-coordinated traffic light, and the driver will denounce the city's traffic engineers for incompetence!

That's only to be expected. Calgarians love their cars, they love driving, and they hate anything that diminishes the driving experience.

Paths

The idea of a pathway along the riverbank seems so perfect, so simple, so easy you might think the paths have always been there.

But such is not the case.

Calgary's marvelous system of riverbank trails was the result of much slow and contentious debate at city hall beginning in the mid-'60s. There were property rights to consider. There was the cost of clearing the overgrown bush

Skates, bikes and jogging shoes share pathways

away along some parts of the riverbanks and the cost of paving and lighting the paths.

Yet, ever so slowly, it happened. The first link was downtown along the north side of the Bow. Prince's Island Park was fixed up, and the scrap yard and warehouses at the site of old Fort Calgary were cleared away.

The paths created strips of parkland along the riverbanks. They became bright green arteries bringing new life to the downtown core. As the years passed, the arteries grew and were extended throughout the city. In their busiest sections, the pathways have been doubled and tripled so cyclists, runners, and strollers can all

Quick Run

THE HEART OF Calgary's pathway system is Prince's Island Park. It's the centrepiece, the setting that shows the most dramatic and most beautiful views of the city skyline.

It's the ideal place for the corporate traveler to go for a run, to work out the frustrations of the business day, and to see the city at its finest. It's a popular pastime. On warm summer lunch hours, the sidewalks leading to the island are crowded with office workers in shorts and running shoes.

There's no set route, but the most charming paths are along the Bow between the Langevin Bridge (4th Street East) and the Louise Bridge (10th Street West). Go upstream on one side of the Bow and return on the other to get the full workout.

Kids in Calgary

CALGARY IS A young city with a high proportion of young families. So it's not surprising there are a grand variety of attractions and activities especially for children. Here are some of the best:

The Zoo

Zoo comes last in the alphabet but always comes first in the hearts of children all over the world.

The Calgary Zoo, Botanical Garden and Prehistoric Park is open every day of the year. As well, unique regular programs are presented for children, including all-night sleep-over parties during summer holidays and other special times during the year.

For details about special events, call 232-9353; for general information, call 232-9372.

Science Centre

The secrets of the stars and all other aspects of science are pre-

Look how high I am!

sented daily. Special hands-on exhibitions and activity areas are in the exhibit gallery while star and laser shows are presented in the planetarium's star chamber.

The Alberta Science Centre/Centennial Planetarium is at 7th Avenue and 11th Street SW. For current show information, call 221-3700.

Leisure Centres

Calgary has not one but two huge public swimming pools making their own waves. Both the Southland Leisure Centre and the Village Square Leisure Centre have wave pools, giant water slides, hot pools, and wading areas. As well, there are hockey arenas, basketball courts, and weight rooms with scheduled activities for every age.

The Southland Leisure Centre is at 2000 Southland Drive SW. Call 251-3505. The Village Square Leisure Centre is at 2623 26th Street NE. Call 280-9714.

Calaway Park

Just a short drive west (a mere 10 kilometers) along the Trans-Canada Highway is Calgary's premiere amusement park.

Calaway Park comes alive with clowns, magicians, and musical entertainers each summer. There are almost two dozen exciting rides, a petting zoo, an amazing get-lost-forever-if-you-want-to maze, games and special events throughout the season. For times, call 240-3824.

Heritage Park

Now here's a blast from the past. Heritage Park gives young and old a glimpse of what life was like in the olden days. With a focus on life for pioneers before 1914, the park presents a variety of programs throughout the year and is open daily during the summer months. There are antique carnival rides, ice cream cones, authentic horse-drawn carriages, the Moyie sternwheeler, and real live steam trains.

The park, situated on a prominent point overlooking the scenic Glenmore reservoir, is at 1900 Heritage Drive SW. For information, phone 259-1900.

Neighborhood Parks & Pools

Almost every residential district in Calgary has a neighborhood playground, complete with ball diamond, a set of swings, or a swimming or wading pool. One of the oldest and most popular kid places is Riley Park in the Hillhurst district. On a hot summer day, there's hardly a better place to be. For information about parks services, call 268-3888. For recorded information on events, facilities, and parks, call the Playline at 268-2300.

Children's Festival

Each spring late in May, the Calgary International Children's

Kids in Calgary

Calgary is a great place for kids to 'horse around'

Festival presents a week-long celebration featuring dozens of performers from around the world. The performances take place at the Calgary Centre for Performing Arts and at the Glenbow Theatre. Outdoor events are held at the Olympic Plaza. For details, call 294-7414.

Museum Amusements
Throughout the year, the Glenbow Museum presents a variety of unique programs especially for children. Young historians can dress up in real knight's armor or feel the softness of a genuine beaver pelt. For information, phone 237-8988.

Clowns always bring a smile

proceed in safety.

Major financial support for the trails came from the Devonian Foundation set up by the late Eric L. Harvie. A pathway bridge, spanning the Bow in Carburn Park, was named after Harvie to commemorate his generous donations.

Each summer the Calgary Police Service issues reminders to cyclists, warning them not to speed on the paths. As well, all bikes must be equipped with bells to warn pedestrians. The trails—all 210 kilometres of them—are often patrolled by police on bicycles or on horseback.

These pathways are now popular recreational areas at all times of the year—and at all hours of the day and night. Even on the coldest winter days, on the paths there are runners bundled up in layers of sweatshirts and pants, wearing toques, scarves—and running shoes.

Golf

Calgary is blessed with a terrific selection of golf courses. It's always been a great golf town and has several members-only private courses that are among the finest in Canada. Calgarians have been hiking in pursuit of the white ball since 1897 when the Calgary Golf and Country Club was founded. The first Country Club was a scruffy piece of pasture between the downtown core and Stampede Park. The members moved to the current picturesque location along the Elbow River in 1911.

Alas, the Country Club is for members only, and green fee players are not allowed. What's more, there is now an 18-year-long waiting list for memberships.

Calgary's first public

Calgary is a city of golfers

course opened at Shaganappi Point in 1915. A total of 2,153 golfers played the course that year. There would have been more, but the parks department spent the summer get-

Grant MacEwan

GRANT MACEWAN is one of Calgary's most inspiring citizens. He was Calgary's mayor. He was a Member of the Legislative Assembly and leader of the provincial Liberal Party. He was the lieutenant-governor of Alberta.

He was farmer and rancher, woodcarver and after-dinner speaker, university professor and dean of agriculture, and he was a lifelong teacher. He was even an honorary fire chief.

As an non-stop author, he told the story of Western Canada by writing a shelf of more than 50 books.

He even acquired a fortune—and gave it away. "I lost my

ambition to make a million dollars," he said. "I thought I was making a mistake letting my money pile up." He presented $601,000 to the Calgary Foundation, which disposes of the interest the funds earn, mostly to environmental conservation groups.

MacEwan was born in 1902 near Brandon, Manitoba, and came to Calgary at the age of 50. He had just lost an election as well as his job; here he built a new life for himself. He built well. His books are a lasting legacy for all Canadians.

Writing is his greatest pleasure. He's still at it, turning out book after book, year after year.

Entertainment hotspots present a great range of evening attractions

ting the fairways in shape, so players weren't allowed on the nine-hole course until the 7th of August. It was a Saturday. Since then, summer weekends in Calgary have never been the same.

Shaganappi Point (almost everyone calls it "Shag") now has 27 holes and, as a bonus, just happens to be one of the finest viewpoints for looking down on the downtown office skyline.

Courses

Confederation Golf Course (9 holes) 3204 Collingwood Drive NW (974-1800): 3221 yards, par 36, city-run, book through 221-3510.

Country Hills Golf Course (9 holes public) 9703 Centre Street North (274-9100): 3500 yards, par 36, book two days in advance.

Elbow Springs Golf Course (18 holes) Springbank (246-2800): 6908 yards, par 72, rating 71.6, slope 119, book three days in advance.

Douglasdale Golf Club (18 holes) 7 Douglas Woods Drive SE (279-7913): 4300 yards, par 60, rating 59.5, slope 106, book four days in advance.

Elks of Calgary Golf and Country Club (18 holes) 2502 - 6th Street NE (276-5040): 6850 yards, par 72, rating 72.9, slope 131, book one day in advance.

Fox Hollow Golf Course (18 holes) 999 - 32nd Avenue NE (277-4653): 6500 yards, par 72, rating 70.2, slope 121, indoor driving range available year-round.

Heather Glen Golf Course (18 holes) 100th Street and Glenmore Trail SE (236-4653): 6399 yards, par 72, rating 70.8, slope 124, book three days in advance.

Inglewood Golf and Curling Club (18 holes) 34th Avenue and Barlow Trail SE (299-9666): 6218 yards, par 71, rating 69.4, slope 120, book two days in advance.

Lakeview Golf Course (9 holes) 5840 - 19th Street SW (974-1815): 1612 yards, par 30, city-run, book through 221-3510.

Maple Ridge Golf Course (18 holes) 1240 Mapleglade Drive SE (974-1825): 6576 yards, par 72, rating 72, city-run, book through 221-3510.

McCall Lake Golf Course (27 holes) 1600 - 32nd Avenue NE (974-1805): 6788 yards, par 71, rating 71.5, city-run, book through 221-3510.

Richmond Green Golf Course (9 holes) 2539 - 33rd Avenue SW (974-1820): 1214 yards, par 27, city-run, book through 221-3510.

Shaganappi Point Golf Course (27 holes) 1200 - 26th Street SW (974-1810): 5284 yards, par 69, rating 66, city-run, book through 221-3510.

Valley Ridge Golf and Country Club (27 holes) 11618 Valley Ridge Park NW (288-9457): 6642 yards, par 72, rating 71.2, slope 126, book one day in advance but by Thursday for weekends.

Nightlife

The big problem with nightlife in Calgary is there's so much of it. How to choose? Ah, such a problem.

Virtually every night of the year, there are theatrical performances, musical concerts, nightclub acts, tavern shows—everything from strippers to symphonies. There's something for every taste and every age group.

For current listings, consult the 'What's Up' section published in the *Calgary Herald* each Friday, the entertainment section of the *Calgary Sun*, or the listings in *Where Calgary Magazine*.

Music

Music, music, music—music for dancing, music for dining, music for experiencing celestial bliss. Select a category and take your pick:

Alternative

The headquarters of the post-grunge gig is The Republik, 219 - 17th Avenue SW. Call 244-1884 to find out which acts are "all ages" and which serve alcohol. Alternatively, there's also the Ship & Anchor Pub at 534 - 17th Avenue SW (245-3333) or the Night Gallery Cabaret, 1209 - B 1st Street SW (264-4484).

Blues

King Edward Hotel, 438 9th Avenue SE, is a must. Blues bars come. Blues bars go. But the good old Eddie remains true blue after all these years. Call 262-1680 to find out which blues legend is playing tonight. If you're lucky, it could be Calgary's own guitar wizard Ellen McIlwaine or basement-voiced Amos Garrett.

Country

Some nights there are so many hat-wearin', boot-kickin', guitar-pickin' acts to choose from it seems Calgary is the country capital of Canada. Uptown country is at Dusty's Saloon, 1088 Olympic Way SE (263-5343). Classic roadhouse country may be found at Ranchman's, 9615 Macleod Trail South (265-1100). Also check Country Roads Saloon at Crossroads Hotel, 2120 16th Avenue NE (291-4666), and Rockin' Horse Saloon, 7400 Macleod Trail South (253-1100).

Mary Dover

MARY DOVER was one of the most wonderful Calgarians ever. She was a soldier and a gardener, as well as the *doyenne* of local society and an alderman, too.

She was born in Calgary in 1905, the daughter of A.E. Cross (brewer, rancher and original Stampede backer) and the former Helen Macleod, whose father was the Mountie Colonel who named Calgary.

In 1930 Mary married Melville Dover and moved to Sri Lanka. When war seemed imminent, she returned to Canada, enlisted and became chief recruiting officer for the Canadian Women's Army Corps. Lieutenant-Colonel Mary Dover, OBE, was the second-highest ranking woman in uniform. After the war, she and her husband lived apart.

She was first elected to city council in 1949. Her political career ended in the 1960s when she moved to a home in the country—and inadvertently disqualified herself from council.

She built a garden there and gave it a Native name, Oksi Hill (meaning "a good place"), on the recommendation of her friend Chief David Crowchild. It became one of the most celebrated landscape gardens in Canada.

Until her death in 1994, she had an active interest in public life and served as honorary colonel of the Steele's Scouts, a historical militia troop.

Bob Edwards

BOB EDWARDS was the most flamboyant and creative soul to dwell in Calgary during the pioneer period.

He was one of Canada's most famous humor writers, yet he never wrote a single book. He was a crusading newspaperman who could never work for a real newspaper. He was an alcoholic, a full-blown drunk, yet he wrote in favor of prohibition.

Bob Edwards was a hilarious gadfly, a thorn in the side to the high and mighty, and a brazen satirist. The articles he wrote for his paper, *The Eye Opener*, made it the most popular publication in Western Canada.

Robert Chambers Edwards was born in Scotland in 1864 into the wrong branch of the prosperous Chambers publishing family. He came to North America in 1892 and, after a couple of false starts in other Alberta towns, finally settled in Calgary in 1904 and began publishing his paper.

Almost from the beginning, *The Eye Opener* was a financial success, even though Edwards was a terrible businessman. The paper was sold from coast to coast, but Edwards was unable to ever get organized enough to sell subscriptions. Instead it was sold on the street by newsboys—but only when Edwards had an issue to sell; far too often he got drunk and missed his deadlines.

His humor seems tame by today's standards, but some of his jokes were regarded as off color by the leading citizens of the day. However, only the guilty were likely to object to the fervor behind his attacks on corruption

and greed.

Perhaps his greatest moment came in the great prohibition debate during the First World War. Despite his notorious reputation as a boozer, Edwards came out strongly against liquor sales. In 1916, Alberta became a dry province as the bars were closed.

Eventually, Bob Edwards achieved respectability. He was even elected to the Alberta legislature in 1921. By then, however, his health was failing. He died in 1922.

The memory of Bob Edwards is kept alive in many ways. A junior high school is named after him, and the popular CBC Radio morning show is called The Eye Opener after his newspaper. As well, each year Alberta Theatre Projects presents a Bob Edwards Award to a distinguished Canadian writer.

The best books about Bob Edwards are *Eye Opener Bob*: *The Story of Bob Edwards* by Grant MacEwan, and *The Best of Bob Edwards* by Hugh Dempsey.

Bob Edwards had an irrepressible sense of wry humor, which he used to fill the columns of his newspaper. Here are some favorite examples of his wit and wisdom:

A little learning is a dangerous thing, but a lot of ignorance is just as bad.

—

We regret to record the sad death of poor Mrs. J. B. Warble of Seventeenth Ave. W. It is said she died of despondency and worry. When the sun didn't shine, deceased was miserable, and when it did, she said that it faded her carpets.

—

Most people who are old enough to know better often wish they were young enough not to.

—

When a man is driven to drink, he usually has to walk back.

—

The many friends of Martin M. Bingham will be sorry to learn that he fell down a steep flight of steps Wednesday and broke his neck. Mr. Bingham was in the act of lowering a case of Three Star Hennessey into the cellar when his foot slipped. It is understood that the Hennessey was three years old and will revert to his widow. The bereaved woman is receiving many callers.

—

Bankruptcy is when you put your money in your hip pocket and let your creditors take your coat.

—

No man ever does as much today as he is going to do tomorrow.

—

Soaking the brain in alcohol does not preserve the mind.

Balloons

ON CALM SUMMER days the sunny, blue sky above Calgary absolutely blossoms with balloons. Lazily, the balloons drift high among the tall buildings. The passengers and pilot wave to the amused office workers and the startled cliff-dwellers in high-rise apartment buildings.

Balloonists fly freely. They float over the rooftops and the trees. They sail across the freeways, the rivers, the creeks, and the Glenmore reservoir. Effortlessly, and with no sound except the occasional blast of the hot-air burner, they even fly above the birds. On one side they see the unsuspecting sunbather on a secluded balcony. On the other

they see the left fielder hurl the ball to home at the neighborhood diamond.

Ballooning could take off in a big way almost anywhere, but the taste for high-altitude, hot-air adventure is stronger in Calgary than any other city in North America, perhaps even the world. There are upwards of 40 licensed balloon pilots and 10 private companies that fly passengers over the city. There is also a balloonists' club which will celebrate its 20th anniversary in 1995.

A grand balloon race is part of the daily grandstand show at the Stampede. The balloons are inflated on the rodeo infield, then take off over the city and into the countryside. It's the one race the entire city can watch. It's a spectacular sight because the balloons come in all sizes and shapes. Some look

like giant shopping carts, some like dinosaurs or houses. Even the ordinary round ones are as colorful as party hats.

During the Olympic Games in 1988, there were 138 balloons engaged in daily races. On one morning, the breezes sent them flying directly over the Calgary International Airport. There was a regular schedule of jets prepared to land. The only solution for the air controllers was to instruct all 138 balloonists to climb to 2,000 feet. That way the 737's and other airliners were able to fly directly under the balloons and complete their landings.

A happy combination of factors has contributed to the success of ballooning. For one thing, there is plenty of space in the country for happy landings and very few areas of danger in the region—no great lakes, no oceans, no impenetrable forests. At the same time, the mountains and other natural features provide a variety of landscape to make a flight intensely interesting.

What's even more exciting is the fact that every flight is different. Generally, the balloons take off from large city parks in the early morning or late afternoon when the breezes are best; often the winds are too

Balloons

strong for safe ballooning in mid-day. It depends on the breezes which park is chosen for the take-off. Usually, the pilot will select the one offering the pas-sengers the best views of both the city and the country-

side. Once the balloon is air-borne, a ground crew follows the flight in a truck. The pilot has a radio to keep in constant contact with the truck and with the air-port control tower. The bal-loon is also equipped with a device that makes it show up on the airport radar systems. There are some balloons so small only the pilot can ride, but most commercial bal-loons can carry two to four passen-gers, and some even handle six.

Judicious use of the gas burner gives the pilot a measure of control over the flight. Some-times the wind at a high altitude will be blowing in a different di-rection from that at lower levels. As well, some tall buildings create

a "wind shadow," which can de-flect a balloon. Beyond this, the flight is conducted at the whim of the winds.

Once a landing site is select-ed, the pilot radios the position to the crew in the pursuit truck. After the landing, the passengers partake of a grand tradition in ballooning, one maintained from the very early days in France more than 200 years ago. A bot-tle of champagne is opened and everyone toasts the success of the voyage.

Harold Warner, Balloonist

HAROLD WARNER *has been bal-looning for 20 years. His com-pany, Aero Dynamics, has the largest fleet of hot air balloons in the world.*

Flying in a balloon in Calgary is the most efficient and exciting way to involve yourself in the in-timacy that occurs between this city and nature.

In other words, we've flown over some big cities, and it's fly-ing over a big city, a place like Pittsburgh, that you sort of find yourself moving out into kind of a mattress of trees and fields.

Well, Calgary's much differ-ent because, as soon as you lift

off, you get a real sense of where the mountains are. You lift up over the city, so you get a great sense of the mountains,

and then there's the foothills where there's a lot of wildlife. We have a close relationship with wildlife. What happens is that you move through that space in a balloon slowly enough to take it all in and sort of *feel* it.

It's very special in the sense that you get to be a part of the intimacy between nature and the city. There's no other way to discover it. You can't do it in a car, and you can't do it on a bus or anything like that. You can do it in a balloon.

Folk

Folk music is always alive and well at the intimate Kensington Deli Cafe, 1414 Kensington Road NW (283-0771). As well, watch for weekend concerts presented by various folk clubs. There are several which present concerts at local community halls. The decor is often spartan, but the music is magnificent. As for bluegrass, it isn't quite folk music, but some folks really enjoy it — and most belong to the Foothills Bluegrass Music Society (244-4521), which holds regular concerts.

Jazz

The jazz scene in Calgary has never been better. The best of home-grown talent and the finest of touring acts appear regularly at Calgary clubs. On some warm summer nights, you'd think you were in New Orleans, and on cool fall evenings, you'd think it was Montréal or San Francisco— but no, it's all happening right here, right now. Check 'em

Clear skies and photographer's telephoto lens bring the moon close to the Calgary downtown skyline

Grey Cup

ONE OF THE biggest years in Calgary's sports history was 1948 when the Stampeders Football Club won the Grey Cup for the first time. Alberta was then in the midst of an oil boom, and newly-rich Calgary oil executives were enthusiastic supporters of the team.

The Stamps had a perfect season, winning every game, thanks to the leadership of Les Lear, the coach who also suited up and played on the team when the going was tough. Lear had signed up two key imports from defunct US teams, quarterback Keith Spaith and pass receiver Woody Strode. The pair made the Stampeders the best team Calgary had ever had.

After the Stamps took the western championship, about 200 high-spirited Stamp fans descended on Toronto, where the Grey Cup was held. They came by plane and by train with a chuckwagon, horses, and a cowboy band. Calgarians danced in station lobbies as their train, the Stampeder Special, chuffed its way across the dominion.

The tom-foolery and hi-jinks— which included an impromptu square dance on the trading floor at the stuffy Toronto Stock Exchange—began a tradition of Grey Cup festivities for decades to come.

The fans set up a chuckwagon on the street and served flapjacks. They got the mayor of Toronto on a horse and put a white cowboy hat on his head. A few fans even tried to get a horse and rider into the lobby of the prestigious Royal York Hotel. They failed, but the legend that they succeeded persists to this day.

The Stamps were battling the Ottawa Rough Riders for the Cup. It was a close game until the Stamps pulled the notorious Sleeper Play, a stunt so outra-

out: Cannery Row, 317 10th Avenue SW (269-8889); Kaos Jazz Bar & Bistro, 718 17th Avenue SW (228-9997); McQueen's Upstairs, 317 10th Avenue SW (269-4722); Mona's Kitchen/The Wine Gallery, main floor Bankers Hall at 315 8th Avenue SW on the western end of the Stephen Avenue Mall. Call 290-1090.

Orchestral and Opera

The Calgary Philharmonic is one of Canada's most acclaimed orchestras. A full range of orchestral music is performed in various series throughout the year at Singer Hall in the Calgary Centre for Performing Arts. Call 294-7420 for details.

The Calgary Opera Association (262-7286) presents a series of concerts starring outstanding singers each year. As well, three full operas are presented annually at the Jubilee Auditorium.

The University of Calgary also presents dozens of

Grey Cup

geous a new rule was put into the books to stop it from ever happening again.

Before the ball was snapped on the Ottawa nine-yard line, Stampeder Norm Hill (later a distinguished brain surgeon) drifted away from the scene of scrimmage and stretched out flat at the far side of the field. When play began he got up, loped over the line, and Spaith tossed the ball to him for the touchdown. The final score: Stamps 12, Ottawa 7.

The train ride home was a transcontinental victory parade for the exultant Calgarians. Small

towns all along the CP mainline honored both players and fans. Classes were canceled so schoolchildren could cheer the heroes at the station. Factories and other trains blew their whistles in greeting. Four aircraft from the Suffield military base gave the train a low-level fly-past salute.

Back home the winners were met with a parade and a grand banquet at the Palliser Hotel. It was Calgary's biggest party since the end of the Second World War.

The Stampeders returned to Toronto in 1949 to defend the title but lost to the Montreal Alou-

ettes. It wasn't until 1971 that the Stampeders laid claim to the Cup again. Then Calgary had to wait until 1992 to win for a third time.

But the tradition of enthusiastic volunteer support continued. Calgarians were given a sense of local pride. Their volunteer involvement set them apart from citizens of other Canadian cities. It set Calgary on a course that led directly, four decades later, to Canada's most successful Olympic Games.

Olympic Legacy

OLYMPIC MEMENTOS ARE everywhere in Calgary.

To get to the Olympic Saddledome at Stampede Park, just follow Olympic Way—or ride there on a bus or C-Train car that is decorated with an Olympic symbol.

At the university there's the Olympic Oval, where the speedskating competitions were held, and an Olympic Arch. The university's Olympic Arch is Calgary's most amusing. It's a sculpture of eight people holding up a great arch of sheet steel. There's another Olympic Arch in front of the Eau Claire YMCA near Prince's Island Park. It's much more dignified.

On the western edge of the city, at Canada Olympic Park, known to one and all as COP (sea oh pea), there's the Olympic Hall of Fame. COP has the Olympic ski jumps, luge and bobsled runs, and an Olympic Torch. There's another at McMahon Stadium, where the Olympic Opening and Closing Ceremonies were held. The tallest Olympic Torch in the world is atop the Calgary Tower. Throughout the Games of '88, it shone brightly night and day and warmed the hearts of all who gazed upon it.

Those are the big souvenirs, but there are thousands more, smaller but just as precious. Virtually every Calgarian collected an Olympic lapel pin or two during the Games. In fact, many have dozens of pins, and some have hundreds.

Collecting pins was a great craze. Companies and organizations issued them as souvenirs. The serious collectors kept careful track of which pins were rare and which were not. They knew, for instance, that *Time Magazine* issued 51,000 pins, but the Canadian Ski Patrol issued only 400. Pins were

hot. Collecting pins was a way that anyone, even non-athletic individuals, could get involved in the Olympics. Pins were traded, pins were sold for large sums of cash, and pins were stolen.

Olympic organizers kept a close eye on the pin market. Only authorized groups could use the official Olympic symbol, and those caught issuing an illegal pin soon found themselves having a serious chat with Olympic lawyers. It was even illegal to use the word *Olympic* or the number '88' without permission. It seems downright silly now, but the organizers didn't want anything to happen that would reduce the impact of the Calgary Games.

The largest pin collections today are held by the Glenbow Museum and the Olympic Hall of Fame at Canada Olympic Park. The Glenbow prepared a display with 1,698 pins, then acquired another 150. The Hall of Fame had 671, then received a gift of 2,437 pins and other mementos that had been collected by Calgary businessman Peter Brill.

But far more important than the Olympic pins and the outstanding Olympic athletic facilities was the Olympic Spirit that created an immense feeling of well-being throughout the city. Calgary had just been through turbulent

The most important thing in the Olympic Games is not to win but to take part, just as the most important thing in life is not the triumph but the struggle.

Olympic Games gave city a lasting legacy

times in the early '80s when declining oil prices brought havoc to local business. The city had grown rapidly, and the Olympics gave everyone, new citizens and old, something good to work at together; it gave thousands of volunteers a way to show the world Calgary still knew how to have a good time.

The splendid Olympic facilities will continue to encourage young athletes for many years to come. Athletes will emerge who will set—then break—new world records in their chosen sports at events around the world. Yet the memory of the 1988 Olympic Winter Games at Calgary will never fade. Forever, there will be Calgarians who will look back at '88 and say it was Calgary's finest hour.

musical and other cultural events throughout the year. Call 220-3199 for the latest line-up.

Rock 'n' Roll

Want to rock? In Calgary you can rock around the clock. Here are some rockin' places: The Back Alley, 4630 Macleod Trail South (287-2500); Crazy Horse, 1315 - 1st Street SW (266-1133); Pancho's, 1220 Kensington Road NW (276-7278); The King's Horse Pub, 607 - 11th Avenue SW (262-8806). If the Horse is packed, check out any of the other spots along 11th, which is known as Electric Avenue, the action strip. More rock venues are opening in the Eau Claire entertainment district. Try Joey Tomato's Kitchen (271-3575), the Barley Mill (291-1500), or the newest hotspot, the Hard Rock Cafe (261-8717).

Comedy

Sit down, relax, and laugh yourself silly listening to stand-up at its best. Two venues to choose from: downtown, Jester's Comedy Club, 239 10th Avenue SE (269-6669), and out southeast, try Yuk Yuk's Komedy Kabaret, 5940 Blackfoot Trail SE (252-2253). Reservations recommended. For zany, improvisational theatre, check out the Loose Moose troupe at their elegant entertainment centre, the only one in the world daring to be known as The Simplex, 2003 McKnight Boulevard NE (291-5682).

Casinos

If today's your lucky day, you might want to check out one of Calgary's casinos: Cash Casino Place, 4040 Blackfoot Trail SE (287-1635); River Park Casino, 1919 Macleod Trail South (266-4355); or Stampede Casino in the Big Four Building at Stampede Park (261-0422).

Recreation Centres

THERE'S NO EXCUSE to get out of shape with the range of fitness facilities available in Calgary.

Eau Claire YMCA

The new Y building, at 101 - 3rd Street SW, is set like a jewel at the main entrance to Prince's Island Park. It features two pools, a fully-equipped gymnasium, racquet and squash courts, a spectacular running track, weight rooms, fully-equipped steam rooms, and other fitness facilities for men and women. Call 269-6701 for drop-in rates and times.

YWCA 320 - 5th Avenue SE

Don't ask why Calgary has a YW just a few blocks away from the YM, just enjoy. The YW is smaller, but well-equipped with gymnasium and pool, as well as courts for squash and racquetball. These are facilities for both men and women. Child care is also available. Call 232-1576 for rates and times.

Lindsay Park Sports Centre

The Centre at 2225 Macleod Trail South hardly needs a sign, because the tent-like facility is such a landmark. Inside there's a cushioned running track, Olympic-size pools, weight rooms and squash courts. Call 233-8619 for times and rates or 233-8393 for taped information.

Leisure Centres

Leisure is hardly the word, if you think *leisure* means relaxing. These centres, operated by the city's parks and recreation department, have everything from weight rooms to hockey rinks. The big attractions are the pools—which are so sophisticated they make their own waves. In the north there's the Village Square Leisure Centre at 2623 - 56th Street NE, which features the Pepsi Thunder Run, a 173-metre long waterslide created in co-operation with a popular soft drink company. Call 280-9714 for information.

Similar facilities, but without the Thunder Run, are in the south. One is Southland Leisure Centre, 2000 Southland Drive SW. Call 251-3505. The other is Family Leisure Centre, 11150 Bonaventure Drive SE. Call 278-7542.

Olympic Oval

The Oval, on the U of C campus, 2500 University Drive NW, is where the Olympic speedskating competitions were held in 1988. Now anyone can skate there in winter or play tennis in summer. Call 220-7954 for details.

University of Calgary

You don't need to be a student. You can dive right in and get in the swim, play racquetball, run, climb the unique three-storey climbing wall, or weight-train. The athletic centre also rents equipment. Call 220-6942 for taped information or 220-7241 for further details.

5. Calendar of Events

Harvey the Hound is popular mascot for the Flames hockey team

January
- *New Year's Day* (holiday).
- *Public skating,* Olympic Plaza daily 9 am to 9 pm.
- *Playrites,* annual festival of new plays presented by Alberta Theatre Projects, Martha Cohen Theatre.

February
- *Calgary Winter Festival,* 10 days and nights family-oriented fun beginning mid-month. Starts with a parade and features snow sculpture contests, races, dances, and feasts.

March
- *Rodeo Royale,* Stampede Corral, Stampede Park. Rodeo at its finest. Held the third week and culminating with final competition on Sunday, as well as the crowning of Stampede Queen and her princesses.

April
- *Cannons, Calgary's Triple A Baseball,* boys of summer launch season mid-month even if the weather is less than summery.

May
- *Native Awareness Week* takes place mid-month, features free performances at Olympic Plaza.
- *International Children's Festival.* Zillions of performers from all over the universe at Calgary Centre for Performing Arts.
- *Heritage Park,* opens for season in time for 24th of May holiday weekend.
- *Lilac Festival* , end of the month, treat your nose to the sweet-scent along 4th Street SW in the Mission District. From 17th Avenue to the Elbow River, residents

Stampede family fun in July

and merchants present one of Calgary's finest neighborhood festivals.

June

- *Kite Day,* a Sunday in late June the sky above South Glenmore Park is alive with kites of all sizes. Be there or be earthbound.
- *Jazz Festival,* biggest names in jazz booked for concerts at various clubs in late June and early July. Watch for free performances at Olympic Plaza and Prince's Island.
- *Carifest,* annual extravaganza of Caribbean-style music and food, takes place at a variety of venues around town. Be sure to catch the weekend events on Prince's Island.

July

- *1 Canada Day* (holiday), a wonderful excuse for a day of partying at Prince's Island.
- *Calgary Stampede,* World's Greatest Outdoor Show on Earth, takes over entire city for almost two weeks during first part of the month. There's nothing else quite like it anywhere.
- *Calgary Folk Festival,* around mid-month, relax from all the rootin' tootin'. Events (some free) held at various locations for five days and nights.
- *Old Bridgeland Days,* sponsored by Bridgeland Riverside Community Association, has best community-event parade, featuring multitude of floats, horses, dogs, clowns, mascots, and antique automobiles. Late in July.

August

- *Heritage Day,* first Monday

(civic holiday), grand party at Prince's Island. A great way to celebrate Calgary's cultural diversity.
- *Bluesfest,* the annual festival of the blues, features a series of free concerts and culminates with a grand evening concert in mid-month.
- *Afrikadey,* a festival to celebrate African music and culture, takes place over five days at a variety of venues in mid-month. Some events free.

September

- *Labor Day* (holiday), first Monday, date for the annual confrontation between the Calgary Stampeders Football Club and their arch enemies, the Edmonton Eskimos.
- *The Masters,* second week of the month, a celebration of the finest equestrian competitions at Spruce Meadows.
- *Artweek* starts in mid-month. Every art gallery holds an open house. This is the art-lovers best opportunity to see what local galleries have to offer.

October

- *Public skating* starts at city rinks. Call 268-3888 for times.
- *Thanksgiving Day,* second

Downtown mall district is always full of surprises

Monday (holiday).
- *31 Hallowe'en,* costumed Calgary kids cruise for candy.

November

- Heritage Park, every weekend until Christmas, special family-oriented events.
- 11 Remembrance Day (holiday).

December

- *Public skating,* Olympic Plaza daily 9 am to 9 pm.
- *Santa Claus,* first Saturday arrives at noon for a grand parade on Stephen Avenue Mall, ending up at Olympic Plaza.
- *25 Christmas* (holiday).
- *26 Boxing Day* (holiday).
- *31 New Year's Eve—First Night Festival.* Family fun from 6 pm to 1 am as Calgarians welcome the New Year.

6. Downtown

Calgary is blessed with one of the most attractive and compact downtown districts of any city its size in the world. It's great strolling territory. There is still a fine stock of pioneer architecture—finely-detailed buildings made of brick, sandstone and terra cotta—as well as many

fabulous glass towers that would stand tall in any city.

There are fine streetscapes, elegant shops, and an abundance of recreation areas and peaceful parkland close at hand.

Calgary Tower

The most striking structure in the heart of the city is the Calgary Tower. Standing dramatically at the point where Centre Street meets 9th Avenue, it's 190 metres high. Contained within the Tower top are the Observation Terrace, Tops Bar & Grill, and the Panorama Dining Room (which is, of course, a very *high*-class restaurant). There's no problem seeing it all when you're

dining at the Panorama. The tables are set on a special floor which revolves once every hour. For reservations and admission details, call 266-7171.

When the Tower was built in 1968, there was nothing taller on the skyline. As soon as it opened, there was a round of housecleaning on the roofs of neighboring downtown building. Heaps of old lumber and rubbish hidden from sight on the roofs had suddenly been brought into public view. Some businesses even went so far as to paint big advertising slogans on their roofs for the sake of the sightseers and diners in the Tower.

The building boom of the 1970s and early '80s brought

forth a battalion of shiny new office towers to challenge the Tower's top spot on the city skyline. The first to surpass it was Petro-Canada Centre, the reddish-brown edifice just a couple of blocks north of the Tower. Now there is such a thicket of tall office buildings it is possible, from some angles, to lose sight entirely of the Calgary Tower.

Even so, the view from the top of the Tower is astonishing. The distant Rockies look superb, but there are sights to see in every direction. Some lucky Calgarians are able to pick out their own homes by using the telescopes on the Observation Terrace. It's even fun to see what's going on in

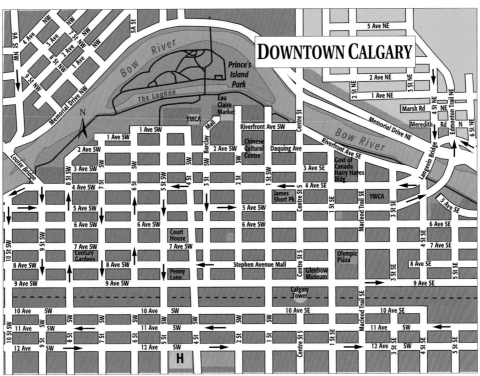

Network of one-way streets makes it easy to get around downtown district

the nearby office buildings. From so high, the cars on the streets and the trains on the CP mainline just below the Tower look like toys.

The spire on top of the Tower was modified for the 1988 Olympic Games. A special natural gas-fired cauldron was set in place which transformed the Tower into the tallest Olympic Torch in history. During the Games in 1988, the Tower Torch was kept lit night and day. Finally it was extinguished during the official Closing Ceremonies.

Now the Torch is lit only on special occasions.

Devonian Gardens

In the heart of the downtown shopping district is an oasis of garden greenery pleasant even on the stormiest day.

Devonian Gardens is Calgary's largest indoor green space. The hectare-sized park is safe beneath a glass roof on the fourth floor of Toronto-Dominion Centre. It fills virtually an entire city block from 7th to 8th Avenues between the Bay and Eaton's, the main retail anchors downtown.

Devonian Gardens is stocked with 20,000 plants of 138 varieties. The exotic plants were specially chosen to match, as much as possible, the trees and bushes that thrive outdoors in the Calgary region; for instance, there are plenty of leafy fig trees resembling the common poplar.

There are also fountains, miniature waterfalls, a children's play area, and plenty of benches for enjoying the scenery. As well, areas have been set aside for art exhibitions, music recitals, and story-telling. Admission is free.

Police Museum

Calgary's newest downtown attraction is a small museum that isn't a museum at all—

LRT

CALL IT THE LRT for Light Rail Transit. Or call it the C-Train because it's Calgary's train.

But remember this—the train is free only in the downtown core from the City Hall station all the way to 8th Street West.

Valid tickets are required outside the downtown area.

Accommodation

WHEN FAMOUS COUNTRY singer Wilf Carter was just a struggling troubadour, he once spent the night under the Langevin Bridge downtown. It was Stampede Week. All the hotels were booked solid and, to tell the truth, young Wilf didn't have much in his pockets in those days; his Nashville hits were only dreams then.

Today, it would be easier. There are plenty of hotels, motels, hostels, and bed & breakfast operations to suit every budget. Here is a selection:

Downtown
Delta Bow Valley, 209 - 4th Avenue SE (266-1980); Elbow River Inn, 1919 Macleod Trail SE (269-6771); International Hotel, 220 - 4th Avenue SW (265-9600); Palliser Hotel, 133 - 9th Avenue SW (262-1234); Prince Royal Inn, 618 - 5th Avenue SW (263-0520); Radisson Plaza Hotel, 110 - 9th Avenue SE (266-7331); Ramada Hotel, 708 - 8th Avenue SW (263-7500); Sandman Hotel, 888 - 7th Avenue SW (237-8626); Stampeder Inn, 3828 Macleod Trail South (243-5531); Westin Hotel Calgary, 320 - 4th Avenue SW (266-1611); Westward Inn, 119 - 12th Avenue SW (266-4611).

South
Best Western Hospitality Inn, 135 Southland Drive SW (278-5050); Blackfoot Inn, 5940 Blackfoot Trail SE (252-2253); Carriage House Inn, 9030 Macleod Trail South (253-1101); Flamingo Motel, 7505 Macleod Trail South (252-4401); Glenmore Inn, 2720

Hospitality awaits the visitor

Glenmore Trail SE (279-8611); Holiday Inn Macleod Trail, 4206 Macleod Trail South (287-2700); Howard Johnson Hotel, 4510 Macleod Trail South (224-1700); Travelodge Macleod Trail, 9206 Macleod Trail South (253-7070).

Northwest
Avondale Motor Inn, 2231 Banff Trail NW (289-1921); Best Western Village Park Inn, 1804 Crowchild Trail NW (289-0241); Budget Motor Inn, 4420 - 16th Avenue NW (288-7115); Crowchild Inn, 5353 Crowchild Trail NW (288-5353); Econolodge, 2440 - 16th Avenue NW (289-2561); Econolodge, Highway 1 at 101st Street (288-4436); Highlander Motel, 1818 - 16th Avenue NW (289-1961); Royal Wayne Motor Inn, 2416 - 16th Avenue NW (289-6651); Super 8 Motel, 1904 Crowchild Trail NW (289-9211).

Northeast
Best Western Port o' Call Inn, 1935 McKnight Boulevard NE (291-4600); Chateau Airport, 2001 Airport Road NE (291-2600); Quality Airport Inn, 4804 Edmonton Trail NE (276-3391); Holiday Inn Calgary Airport, 1250 McKinnon Drive (230-1999); Marlborough Inn, 1316 - 33rd Street NE (248-8888); Pointe Inn, 1808 - 19th Street NE (291-4681); Sheraton Cavalier Hotel, 2620 - 32nd Avenue NE (291-0107).

Hostel
Calgary International Hostel, 520 - 7th Avenue SE (269-8239).

Bed and Breakfast
B&B on the Bow, 23 New Bow Lane SE (263-6769); Chinook Park, 7812 Churchill Drive SW (259-6592); The Crescent, 635 Crescent Boulevard SW (287-0654); Inglewood Bed & Breakfast, 1006 - 8th Avenue SE (262-6570); Lions Park Bed and Breakfast, 1331 - 15th Street NW (282-2728); Russell's Bed & Breakfast, 2806 Linden Drive SW (249-8675); Turgeon's Bed and Breakfast, 4903 Viceroy Drive NW (288-0494).

The Bed and Breakfast Association of Calgary has details on 40 member homes. For information call 274-7281 between 8 am and 6 pm.

The Calgary Convention & Visitors Bureau also has information. Phone 263-8510. Out of town call toll-free 1-800-661-1678. If they can't help you, well, there's always a bridge. . . .

even though it looks like a museum and everyone calls it a museum. Technically, it's the Calgary Police Service Interpretive Centre. It's located on the second floor at the old main police station at 316 - 7th Avenue SW.

The centre includes displays that focus on the crimes and social issues Calgary police officers must deal with daily. There is a reconstruction of Calgary's pioneer jail, a courtroom, and a dingy dead-end flophouse that looks frighteningly real.

As well, there are exhibits of various "tools of the trade" used by the police service over the years, including a modern patrol car and an antique Harley-Davidson motorcycle.

For details, call 266-4565.

Sunshine always follows the sudden summer shower

Downtown Restaurants

RESTAURANT CRITIC John Gilchrist's recommendations for the downtown area:

The Owl's Nest at the Westin Hotel, 4th Avenue & 3rd Street SW (266-1611), certainly is the best of the best as far as elegant hotel dining goes. The second one would be the **Conservatory** in the Delta Hotel, 209 - 4th Avenue SE (266-1980). Too, the **Rimrock Room** at the Palliser, 133 - 9th Avenue SW (262-1234), is always a pleasant place.

I think Chinatown is a time-locked place. Many restaurants are in the old Cantonese style with reminders of the pineapple chicken ball era. But there is a new move happening in Chinatown with places like the **Grand Isle**, 128 - 2nd Avenue SE (269-7783), which bring you a contemporary Cantonese style. It's fresher, lighter, more flavorful,

and it incorporates a bit more of the Szechuan or Peking style of spicing.

Things are really changing along the Stephen Avenue Mall. The places that were tacky t-shirt shops are turning into interesting restaurants. There's the new **Gold Coast Cafe**, 109 Stephen Avenue SW (233-7290), which is Calgary's first West African restaurant. The food is frequently chicken and meatballs, but, on occasion, you can get fufu, which is a wonderful West African mashed potato dish. Also on the Stephen Avenue Mall, you'll find the **Beirut**, 112 Stephen Avenue SW (264-8859), with a modest decor but very good Lebanese food. **Mona's** in Bankers Hall, 315 - 8th Avenue SW (290-1090), is very good for the quick soup-and-sandwich business lunch.

We can't ignore the **Calgary**

Tower, 101 - 9th Avenue SW (266-7171). The quality of food in the Panorama Room has significantly improved over the past five or six years.

Other places include: **Divino's**, 817 - 1st Street SW (263-5869), for its contemporary California style of cuisine and **Teatro**, 200 - 8th Avenue SE (290-1012). The historical restoration of the building is great. The food might be a bit pricey, but it's good.

At the Eau Claire Market, the best of the best is **Cajun Charlie's**, 200 Barclay Parade SW (233-8101), with its Cajun cuisine. Most establishments at Eau Claire are best for an after-work beer, but Cajun Charlie's is the one place where I'd go out of my way to dine.

Plus-15 and The Mall

Plus-15? What's a Plus-15? Well, Plus-15 is certainly a funny name for it, but that's what Calgarians call a second-storey, pedestrian walkway that crosses a downtown street in mid-air and in mid-block.

Calgary has so many of them—54 at last count and more coming—that the city is the Plus-15 capital of the world.

The curious name came from 1970 when the first Plus-15 pedestrian bridge was built. That was long before the country made the shift to the metric system. Theoretically, a Plus-15 is 15 feet above the street level. That's about five metres—so, in a perfect metric world, a Plus-15 might be called a High 5.

No matter what they're called, though, the pedestrian bridges have proven to be a grand success. Even on the coldest days, it's now possible to stroll in comfort from one building to another without bundling up.

The Plus-15 bridges are connected to well-marked pathways going right through department stores and office towers. There are now some 12 kilometres of internal corridors in the downtown district.

In the shopping district, the Plus-15 level is a busy retail area and looks like one huge, non-stop, fancy shopping mall. In the business areas, it's much more sedate. In both areas, though, there are plenty of fast food take-out restaurants. At noon, it's hard to find a seat at most of the food courts.

In the Bow Valley Square complex, there is even a live stage theatre on the Plus-15 level. Called, appropriately, Lunchbox Theatre, it specializes in noon-hour, dramatic plays and musicals. For information about current shows, call 265-4292.

Stephen Avenue Mall

Downtown, "the Mall" is different from shopping malls in the suburbs. Suburban retail malls are interior spaces, but the Stephen Avenue Mall is the real thing. It's outdoors, and it's Calgary's most historic street, lined by a collection of some of the best preserved buildings from the pioneer era to be found anywhere in Western Canada.

Stephen Avenue was the original name for 8th Avenue. The name was bestowed by the real estate division of the Canadian Pacific Railway. At first all the downtown streets had names. Centre Street was McTavish, 9th Avenue was Atlantic, and 10th was Pacific. When city council dropped the names and began the system of numbers in 1904, it was the

Witold Twardowski

WITOLD TWARDOWSKI has been creating popular restaurants, resorts, and mountain lodges for more than 20 years. When he's not working at one of his several nightspots, he likes to travel in tropical climes.

It's not completely by choice that I'm a restaurateur. I kind of fell into it then and I continue to fall. I guess I see myself as a little bit more of an adventurer and poet. The whole notion of *restaurant* for me is not just food. It's an amalgamation of all sorts of different things that I've experienced, that are somehow logged into my psyche. Then I see someplace, a specific site, usually an older building, which triggers some kind of recognition of something that is laying within these walls and what it could be.

So, Mescalero was very much out of a series of trips to Mexico, the Southwest and South America. The fire, and the subsequent destruction and distress of the building, gave it a several-hundred-year-old patina, along with the archways that were already there. It was reminiscent of 'Anywhere, Latin America,' two or three hundred years old. So the menu is a poetic interpretation of, you know, cowboys and Indians and Latinos, in some time warp.

I have a picture in my mind of what it should look like, so my job is to make sure that the staff understands it, and that they do it. I love my own places and I spend a lot of time in them.

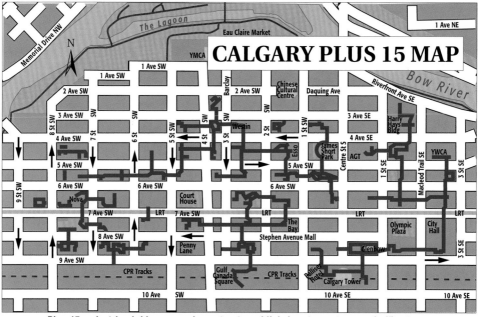

CALGARY PLUS 15 MAP

Map labels: The Lagoon, Memorial Drive NW, Eau Claire Market, 1 Ave NE, YMCA, Barclay, Chinese Cultural Centre, Daquing Ave, Riverfront Ave SE, Bow River, 1 Ave SW, 2 Ave SW, 3 Ave SW, 4 Ave SW, 5 Ave SW, 6 Ave SW, 7 Ave SW, 8 Ave SW, 9 Ave SW, 10 Ave SW, Westin, Esso, James Short Park, Harry Hays Bldg, 3 Ave SE, 4 Ave SE, 5 Ave SW, 6 Ave SW, Centre St S, AGT, YWCA, Macleod Trail SE, 1 St SE, 3 St SE, Court House, LRT, Nova, Stephen Avenue Mall, The Bay, Olympic Plaza, City Hall, Penny Lane, Glenbow, Gulf Canada Square, CPR Tracks, Palliser Hotel, Calgary Tower, 10 Ave SE, 9 St SW, 8 St SW, 7 St, 6 St, 5 St SW, 4 St, 3 St, 2 St, 1 St SW, 2 Ave SW

Plus-15 pedestrian bridges cross busy streets and link downtown stores and office towers

next-best thing to a declaration of independence from the powerful railroad, which was then Calgary's only link with the rest of the world.

Two of the original names have been revived to identify the main pedestrian mall system. Stephen Avenue (8th) from City Hall and the Olympic Plaza to 3rd Street West has been re-dubbed Barclay Mall. Ornamental lampposts, planters, benches, and other decorative fixtures have been installed along the pedestrian malls, but the real showpieces are the old buildings along the Stephen Avenue Mall.

For a short walking tour, start at Olympic Plaza and head west. Two of Calgary's most distinguished old buildings face the Plaza. The Burns Building and the Calgary Public Building form book-ends for the Calgary Centre for Performing Arts (CCPA).

The Burns Building, on the east end of the CCPA, was built in 1912. Faced in ornate terra cotta, the building is a monument to Pat Burns, one of the most prosperous ranchers of pioneer days. He operated a meat market on the ground floor; the

59

space is now occupied by a fashionable restaurant and bar. The Public Building, which opened in 1931, was built by the federal government as a reward for voting Conservative. Calgary's most prominent MP, R.B. Bennett, had just become prime minister of Canada. The main floor, once the city's main post office, is now the entrance lobby of the CCPA's Singer Hall.

Facing the Public Building is another prize example of terra cotta architecture, the Dominion Bank Building of 1911, which also is now used by an elegant restaurant and a congenial bar.

Architecture provides visual feast

Immediately west are some of Calgary's finest old buildings, notably the Doll Block at 116 Stephen Avenue SE, which has a distinctive "pot belly" window on the third floor. The building, erected in 1907, was recently

restored to its former elegance from top to bottom to accommodate the offices of the Esther Honens International Piano Competition Foundation and the Calgary International Organ Festival. At 112 is the Thomson Brothers Block, built in 1893. For a great view of the ornamental stonework on the upper floors, walk up to the second level of the Convention Centre on the south side of the street; the staircase is at the entrance to the Glenbow and the Convention Centre.

On the northwest corner of the intersection of Stephen Avenue and Centre Street is one of the most remarkable examples of a complete renovation. The Royal Bank of Canada Building at 102 Stephen Avenue SW was the Hudson's Bay store in pioneer Calgary. Built in sections between 1890 and 1905, it was gutted completely in 1977, and a new interior was constructed;

Plazas near City Hall have become popular centres for variety of family fun events

only the magnificent exterior walls from the original structure were preserved.

The old Ashdown's Hardware block at 110 Stephen Avenue SW dates from 1891 but has been given fresh life with a thorough renovation. For many years the grand facade was obscured by glaring electric signs, and the windows were plugged with inappropriate glass bricks. Now it has been brought back to its former glory as an art gallery.

The folks at the Banke, 125 Stephen Avenue SW, may not know how to spell bank, but they certainly do know how to have a good time. Formerly the head office of the Bank of Nova Scotia and still bearing bank decorations, the Banke is now a popular night club.

At the 1st Street end of the block are two of the most celebrated architectural treasures. On the north side is the former head office of the Bank of Montreal, built in 1930. Now a music and electronics store, it still is emblazoned with the bank's coat of arms in the pediment. Across the Avenue is the Alberta Block, formerly the Alberta Hotel, which dates from 1903. The Alberta was once the premier hotel in Calgary and, so goes the legend, had a tavern with the longest bar in all of Western Canada.

Across 1st Street is the massive, landmark Bay store. Further on is a pair of real pioneers—the Lancaster Building at 308 Stephen Avenue, and directly across the Avenue, the old Canada Life Building. The two neighbors are both now directly connected to the much larger office towers that were built beside them.

City Hall

How very strange. One of Calgary's newest hotspots is the City Hall district. It's a great family fun place and the seat of civic government too.

Calgary's City Hall is a sandstone jewel, one of the few civic administration buildings left from pioneer times anywhere in Western Canada. It was opened in 1911 and reflects the grand optimism of the era before the First War.

Standing next to it, like a grand silver showcase, is the new Municipal Building. The main floor of the Municipal Building is the scene of art exhibitions, musical presentations, and other shows. When there's

Glenbow

THERE'S NO EASY way to judge how much time to set aside for a visit to the Glenbow. For a tourist trying to see all of Calgary's important attractions on a quick visit, two or three hours should be enough for the high points.

But for anyone with an abiding interest in western Canadian history, or Canadian art, even an entire day might not be enough. The true fanatic will want to move right in and stay forever.

There is so much to see. The Glenbow has three exhibition floors. One is for art, and two are for ethnological and historical displays. As well, several smaller spaces have been created for smaller shows. Also, the Glenbow often displays touring exhibitions from other museums in Canada, the United States, and elsewhere.

The collections are astounding—in quality and quantity. The Glenbow holds the Victoria Cross won by a Calgary soldier, George Pattison, at Vimy Ridge in the First World War. It has Sitting Bull's pipe. It has an Olympic torch used in 1988 to bring the flame from Mount Olympus in Greece to Calgary for the Winter Games—and it even has the most extensive collection of Olympic commemorate lapel pins, all gathered by Glenbow staffers during the craze of pin-trading at Winter Games events.

The museum's holdings include 200,000 artifacts and artworks, ranging from celebrated paintings to fragile fragments of leather and feather once used as adornments by native people.

*Native artifacts form an
important collection*

As well, there are more than one million historic photographs and negatives. The library has almost 100,000 books and pamphlets, many centuries old. The archives has so many documents they cannot be counted, and so they are measured by the amount of shelf space they occupy. At last tally, there were more than 2,500 running metres of documents.

There are major exhibits on native peoples, the coming of the railroad, military history, and an astonishing collection of exotic rocks and minerals.

The museum's formal name is Glenbow-Alberta Institute, but most folks call it simply "The Glenbow." It began life as a rich

man's private organization. Eric Harvie, Calgary's greatest philanthropist, established the Glenbow Foundation in 1954. From the start it was the most significant resource for historical research in Western Canada.

Eric Harvie was a collector with an insatiable appetite. He even picked up the entire contents of at least six other museums that were closing, and he hired the former owners of one museum to help catalogue the artifacts.

In 1966, the Glenbow became a board-run institution operated by the province. At one time, collections and staffers were scattered among eight buildings. All were united when moved to the current location in 1976.

The Glenbow has an important collection of ethnological artifacts, one of the largest accumulations of native peoples' artifacts in any Canadian museum. Many of the treasures from the collection were part of the *Spirit Sings* exhibition which was the most prominent cultural event associated with the Winter Olympics in 1988.

The hoard acquired by Harvie

Museum

Calgary corporations are strong supporters of Glenbow projects

has been enlarged with the collections gathered by other prominent philanthropists. Oilman Carl O. Nickle donated Canadian and Newfoundland coinage.

Robert M. Borden, chairman of the Bumper Development Corporation, donated an extensive collection of priceless Asian religious sculpture and Eskimo masks. The Bumper donations include masterpiece sculptures of Buddha and other religious figures dating back more than 1500 years.

Norcen Energy Resources Limited donated a collection of 32 modern oil paintings by such masters as Jean-Paul Riopelle, Harold Town, David Milne, and William Kurelek. The Glenbow Museum Acquisitions Society, made up of a group of volunteer fund-raisers, continues to gather financial backing so the museum can purchase additional materials to improve the collections.

The Glenbow is located at 130 - 9th Avenue SE and is open Tuesday through Sunday from 10 am to 6 pm.

something really big happening—like during the medal presentations at the Olympics—hot chocolate and other treats are served in the lobby.

In front of the Municipal Building is the Municipal Plaza, and across the street is an even bigger plaza, the Olympic Plaza. It was here that champion athletes from all over the world were honored during the Games of 1988. Now the Plaza is used for a va-riety of events, from square dancing at Stampede, to ice skating during the winter.

Calgary Centre for Performing Arts

The Calgary Centre for Performing Arts, which faces Olympic Plaza, is the city's one-stop theatre district. Under one roof are three theatres. In the southeast corner is the Max Bell Theatre, home of Theatre Calgary. The Martha Cohen Theatre, the intimate space of Alberta Theatre Projects, dominates the north side of the centre. And tucked in the basement (the door is on the south side next to Theatre Calgary's) is the newest theatre of all, the intimate Engineered Air Theatre, which is used for concerts and performances by a variety of community groups.

At the west end is the grand Jack Singer Hall with its mighty Carthy Organ, home of the Calgary Philharmonic

Eric Harvie

ERIC HARVIE did more for Calgary than any other private citizen in the city's history. Certainly he did more than most politicians. He made it a better place in a multitude of ways, great and small, and did it so quietly even now it is difficult to tally the total of his good works.

That was the way Harvie wanted it. He was a proud man and had his share of little vanities, but he preferred to work in the background and didn't like to draw attention to himself.

He set up private foundations to do the good deeds for him and bankrolled them with the profits from his oil holdings.

He created Heritage Park and gave it to the city. He built the Glenbow Museum and turned it over to the province. He gave so much money to the Calgary Zoo that his wife, Dorothy, was accorded the honour of naming all the Zoo's baby giraffes after her grandchildren.

Harvie was rich, richer than the richest lottery winner. He was always comfortably well-off, and for the last twenty years of his long life, he was one of the wealthiest men in Canada, perhaps *the* wealthiest. Yet he and his family continued to live quietly in a spartan and unassuming manner.

He made his fortune in oil and owned the mineral rights to entire oil fields. Leduc and Redwater in central Alberta were the big ones, but he had smaller holdings scattered all across Western Canada and in the north.

He set up the Glenbow Foundation in 1954, and he named it after his ranch. When the foundation was turned over to the province in 1966, he created the Riveredge Foundation, named after his city home, to continue his collecting habits.

Born in 1892 in Ontario, he moved to Calgary in 1911 and became a lawyer. During the First World War, he enlisted and was wounded in the leg in 1916. He was soon back in action and ended the war with the rank of captain.

Forever after he maintained a strong interest in military matters. During the Second World War, he was commandant of the Calgary Mounted Constabulary, a volunteer, home guard group which assisted both the police and regular armed forces. Later he served as honorary colonel of the Calgary Highlanders.

When he died in 1975, Harvie was actively involved in Glenbow administration and was planning the new home in downtown Calgary for the Glenbow Museum.

No matter how you look at it, the Calgary Tower is at the centre of things

Orchestra.

Hidden in an upper-level corridor is a retail space that has been transformed into the Secret Theatre by the One Yellow Rabbit troupe.

Fort Calgary

Just an eight-minute walk east from City Hall is the place where Calgary began, Fort Calgary Park.

The original fort didn't last long. It was built in 1875 but was judged too scruffy to be left standing by the time the CPR arrived in 1883. The Mounties erected new buildings and remained there until 1914 when the fort site was occupied by a railroad and other industrial operations. Finally, just in time for Calgary's first centennial in 1975, the heavy industries were moved out, and Fort Calgary Park was created.

Today, the old log fort is being reconstructed. There is also an interpretive centre (290-1875), with a small theatre & gallery. As well, Deane House, the house occupied by the last Mountie commissioner, has been converted into a popular tea room (call 269-7747 for reservations).

CHINATOWN IS ONE of Calgary's most popular happy places. Calgarians gather there for good times, especially for good food. Company banquets are held in Chinatown; business deals are negotiated over dim sum lunches; and teenagers in love go to Chinatown for their first formal date.

The restaurants in Chinatown are among the very finest in the world and have been singled out for high praise by the *New Yorker* magazine. The reasons are simple. First of all, fine dining is an essential part of Chinese culture. Calgary has a large and prosperous community that demands good food prepared according

to traditional Chinese methods. And, finally, there are plenty of well-trained chefs to supply it.

Chinatown is also Calgary's most exotic shopping centre, where gourmet cooks go to shop for fancy pickled eggs and where gardeners go to buy the spectacular ceramic pots the eggs came in. It's not large as China-towns

go—nowhere near the size of Chinatown in Vancouver or San Francisco—but it is undoubtedly the largest ethnic-oriented district in Calgary. And it is thriving. Calgary's Chinatown is the largest in the three prairie provinces.

However, Chinatown is much more than an ordinary business or residential district. In a way, it's a living symbol of successful multiculturalism. It proves that there's more

Chinatown

to the image of Calgary than cowpersons and oil companies. Chinatown has been an important part of Calgary's character since the earliest pioneer days.

It's true, though, there have been some sad and nasty chapters in the district's history. The pioneer residents and merchants in Chinatown often endured discrimination based on bigotry, intolerance, and racism. Shamefully, it was not until 1967 that Canadian immigration law treated people from China the same way as those from other countries.

Calgary's first Chinatowns (there were two or three of them, depending on how they are counted) were near the railway tracks. The community moved to its current location at the foot of the Centre Street Bridge just before the First World War. And there it took root and has flourished.

The Canton Block, built in 1910, has always been the main anchor. It's the simple, two-storey, brick building on the east side of Centre Street stretching from 2nd Avenue midway down the block. It seems a humble edifice now, but for decades it was the architectural heart and soul of Chinatown. It was on the main floor of the Canton Block that the leading merchants set up shop; upstairs were living quarters, meeting rooms, and (most important of all) the restaurants. The Canton Block was the cen-

trepiece. Around it grew a neighborhood of homes, businesses, and social organizations.

When it began, Calgary's Chinatown was on the fringe of development, but as time passed, real estate agents and civic planners began to cast covetous eyes at the land. During the 1960s there were plans to replace the Centre Street Bridge and push a major traffic freeway through the very heart of Chinatown. In effect, Chinatown would have been paved out of existence.

The residents fought back. For many of them, the redevelopment plans were just another example of institutional racism. They won many battles and, by 1976, even managed to convince city council to approve a neighborhood revitalization plan.

The greatest demonstration of the new strength of Calgary's Chinatown is the Calgary Chinese Cultural Centre, which opened in 1992.

The $10 million Centre, dominating the intersection of 1st Street and Daqing (2nd) Avenue SW, is a grand showplace topped with a distinctive dome modeled after the Temple of Heaven in Beijing. Beneath the dome are the most-decorated ceiling and walls in Calgary. The gleaming hall is named after Henry Fok, a Hong Kong businessman who contributed $1.5 million to complete the project.

The Centre includes offices of several social agencies as well as a library and meeting rooms set up to encourage trade with China. It also has an exhibition gallery to display art and artifacts from China. Among the treasures on display is a life-size replica grouping of moulded clay soldiers like the famous artifacts excavated from an emperor's grave at Xi An in China. The group was donated by the Chinese government and was brought to Calgary by Victor Mah, a prominent businessman who was founding chairman of the Centre. Mah got the group and a set of stone guard lions from the Chinese Pavilion at Expo '86 in Vancouver.

Corporate Heroes

MONEY JUMPS RIGHT out of the ground and flies straight into the pockets of some Calgarians, or so it seems.

Most of the wealth in recent years has come from oil and gas, but there were millionaires in pioneer days who made their fortunes by dealing in cattle, or timber, or other investments. Some kept their money to themselves, but many have made it a point to share their wealth with others.

None can match the largesse of the late Eric Harvie (see page 64) but dozens have followed the example of former mayor Grant MacEwan (see page 40) who gave a fortune to the Calgary Foundation. Charitable agencies like the Calgary Foundation are able to ensure that the benefits of donations never stop; by investing the sums, they are able to give away the interest earned year after year.

Max Bell

Bell inherited the near-bankrupt *Albertan* newspaper, turned it around, and built an empire based on newspapers, race horses, and oil and gas stocks. When he died in 1972 at age 59, he left the bulk of his estate to local charities. A sports arena in Southeast Calgary and the largest theatre in the Calgary Centre for Performing Arts were named after him to commemorate large donations.

Patrick Burns

Burns was one of the Big Four ranchers who bankrolled the first Stampede in 1912. He was a prosperous meatpacker and left behind a national food products company that still bears his name. When he died in 1937, he set aside money to support children in need, as well as the orphans and widows of police officers and fire fighters. The Burns Memorial Fund continues to help young Calgarians.

Nat Christie

Christie and his brothers ran the old Ontario Laundry, the first large commercial laundry in Calgary. They also raised horses and enjoyed hunting. Nat was a prominent member of the Stampede Board until his death in 1954 at age 81. It was his sister Claire Christie Might who set up the Nat Christie Foundation in 1981; the Christie funds have been put to work at the Calgary Centre for Performing Arts, which has a Christie reception lobby, and by the Alberta Ballet Company, which is housed in the Nat Christie Centre, 141 - 18th Avenue SW.

Harry Cohen

Cohen and his brothers were the first merchants in Canada to recognize the potential of the transistor radio. They made a deal with Sony, and they all became millionaires many times over. As a surprise birthday gift to his wife, Cohen donated $1 million to the Calgary Centre for Performing Arts. The Martha Cohen Theatre was named in her honor.

William Roper Hull

One of the wealthiest men of the pioneer era, Hull is best remembered today because his initials are grandly carved in stone at the entrance of Calgary's most elegant sandstone edifice, the Grain Exchange Building on 1st Street and 9th Avenue SW. The grain exchange failed, but Hull made a fortune anyway in beef, beer, and building supplies. He died in 1925 yet there was enough money remaining in his estate in 1962 to establish the Hull Home (now Hull Child and Family Services) which helps children and families in distress.

Fred Mannix

There has been a Fred Mannix at the head of the Mannix clan for most of the century. The family is one of the most prosperous and most secretive in Western Canada. The first Fred ran the family business, heavy construction, until his death in 1951 at age 70. His son, also Fred,

Corporate Heroes

Many Calgary millionaires found their fortunes in the Alberta oilpatch

expanded into mining and oil, and once was Peter Lougheed's boss. Now the family firm is run by Frederick Philip Mannix. There was a Mannix Foundation, but the name was changed to Carthy Foundation. This foundation donated the Carthy Organ to the Calgary Centre for Performing Arts.

McMahon Brothers

Frank and George McMahon were among the most flamboyant high rollers during the oil boom of the 1950s. Frank ran Pacific Petroleum and WestCoast Transmission, and George was president of the Calgary Stampeders Football Club. The brothers were in their prime when

they donated a football stadium to the city in 1960 and had it built in just 100 days. In thanks, the stadium was named McMahon Stadium.

Nickle Family

Sam Nickle ran a shoe store but got caught up in the oil patch in the early days of the Turner Valley field. His son Carl Nickle was a reporter who began the *Nickle Oil Bulletin*; he was so good he knew about Imperial Oil's first Leduc discovery before the company president did. Carl was later an outspoken member of parliament and established several companies of his own. Sam donated $1 million to create the Nickle Arts Museum at the Uni-

versity of Calgary, and Carl presented the museum with a priceless coin collection. The Nickle Family Foundation continues to disperse funds from the family fortunes.

Jack Singer

Land and buildings made Jack rich. He and his cousin, Abraham Belzberg, began with small buildings in downtown Calgary and built an empire across Western Canada. Jack, now in his 70s, spends much of his time in California, where he is a major player in the Hollywood movie industry. The main concert hall at the Calgary Centre for Performing Arts was named Jack Singer Hall after he made a $1 million donation.

Eau Claire / Prince's Island Park

Good things don't always just happen. The new excitement at Eau Claire and Prince's Island is a case in point. For years Calgary's planners and real estate developers have been fretting about what to do with the area. It took them decades to get going, but finally the results are coming to fruition. The new Eau Claire Market and the continued upgrading of Prince's Island Park have created one of the finest people places in Western Canada. It's fun all year round.

In pioneer days, Prince's Island was an industrial site. It was a sawmill and lumberyard, one of Calgary's first big enterprises. Peter Prince was the mill manager. The mill workers lived nearby and called the area Eau Claire, after the town in Wisconsin where many of them had lived.

It was a vibrant neighborhood including Calgary's major baseball diamond and Buffalo Stadium, as well as the cavernous Civic Garage, used for city vehicles and transit buses. The streets were full of small factories, warehouses, and neatly-kept homes. A few houses were so beautiful, in fact, they were eventually hoisted and taken to Heritage Park.

Over time, factories and warehouses moved out, and the residential neighborhood became a grim wasteland of shabby parking lots. Redevelopment has come slowly but has been welcomed gladly by Calgarians. Prince's Island Park is one of the busiest public spaces in the city. It's *the* place for all the big outdoor festivals. There are ducks to watch, swings for children, and a wonderful summer restaurant, the River Cafe (261-7670), which began life as a lowly hamburger stand, proving once again some things do get better with age.

Now the Eau Claire Market has transformed the district into one of Calgary's most exciting entertainment hotspots. It includes a large-screen IMAX theatre (263-4629) and regular movie theatres, as well as a variety of shops, boutiques, restaurants, and bars.

The Market is built in a high-tech style, with plenty of gleaming ironwork in imitation of the old industrial buildings that once dominated the Eau Claire streetscape. However, there are two authentic reminders of days gone by. One is a towering chimney.

Eau Claire Market is at the heart of Calgary's newest year-round people place

Prince's Island was site of one of Calgary's earliest sawmills; now it's a favorite recreational area

Formerly attached to a boiler house, it's now a sign. The other is a homely old restaurant at 334 Riverfront Avenue SW, which once was the sawmill head office. The restaurant (269-9255) is known by the date the charming old office was built: 1886. 1886 is strictly for day-people. The old front door is closed at 3 pm even though 1886 is surrounded by bars that stay wide-open until even the moon and stars are tired.

Centres with Stories

Science Centre

The Alberta Science Centre/ Centennial Planetarium started, appropriately enough, with its head in the clouds and its eyes firmly focused on the distant stars.

That was in 1967, the year of Canada's Centennial of Confederation. The planetar-

ium was Calgary's largest and fanciest centennial project. Trouble was, after a dozen years or so, attendance at the planetarium's star shows dropped off. The planetarium was running the risk of turning into a white elephant.

Then a new administrative board was set up, and the centre was given a new down-to-earth mandate as a proper science centre. Instead of focusing exclusively on astronomy and outer space, the centre encourages all the sciences, from "virtual reality" computer installations to dinosaur recreations.

As well, there is an intimate theatre space used for concerts and community presentations.

The Alberta Science Centre/Centennial Planetarium is located at 11th Street and 7th Avenue SW. For information, call 221-3700.

Boomtown Ghost

The head office of the Calgary Catholic Board of Education at the corner of 5th Avenue and 9th Street SW is a shiny new building—but it also has a remarkable history.

The 12-storey building was finished in 1993—but for more than a decade it was an unfinished six-storey stump. Originally, it was going to be a regular office tower. Construction began on October 10, 1981, but halted early in '82 when the developer went broke. It was the city's most prominent monument to the abrupt end of the oil boom. For years cynics called it the Boomtown Ghost.

It was a mess. Rusty iron bars poked out of dirty, grey concrete. Brown brick siding was unfinished and looked as if the bricklayers might return after their coffee break. City commissioners wanted to call

Alberta Science Centre/Centennial Planetarium was opened in 1967 to commemorate Canada's 100th birthday

in a wrecking crew to get rid of the eyesore.

Finally, the derelict skeleton was rescued by the school board. First they checked to see if the structure was still safe. There were fears that a decade of rain and snow had weakened the network of cables supporting the concrete floors. Engineers used X-ray cameras to check the cables and replaced several that were damaged. Then the top six floors were built. The wiring was improved for computers, and the original brick siding was removed in favor of energy-efficient polished granite and reflective metal panels.

While it had been abandoned, the building had been entered by vandals who put graffiti on walls and pillars, including some shocking Satanic messages. Before work began, a painter eradicated the evil graffiti, and a priest conducted a rite of exorcism.

McDougall Centre

This handsome sandstone edifice at 455 - 6th Street SW is the main southern base for the premier and other provincial government officials. As the inscription on the building's east side declares, the structure began as McDougall School in 1906. The school was named after a prominent pioneer family; George McDougall and his son John were both Methodist missionaries who moved west from Ontario in 1863.

The building served for many years as a Normal School, a training centre for teachers, then was used as an ordinary neighborhood school, then finally as the headquarters of the Calgary Board of Education's public school system.

Eventually, however, it was taken over again by the provincial government and given a thorough restoration in 1982. The old classrooms were converted into offices and meeting rooms, and an underground parking garage was put under the old playground. To complete the centre, the grounds were extensively re-landscaped. It is now a popular place for outdoor concerts in the summer. For tour information, call 297-8687.

Energeum

You will look in vain for the word *Energeum* in the dictionary. There's only one, and there's nothing quite like it anywhere else in the world. The Energeum, at 640 - 5th Avenue SW, does nothing but tell the story of Alberta's energy industries. There's a hands-on display of sticky oil sands from northern Alberta (don't worry, Mom, rubber gloves are attached to the showcase) and exhibits that show how oil and gas were formed back in the days of the dinosaurs.

Speaking of dinosaurs, there's even a well-preserved, real-life dinosaur—namely, a shiny, gas-guzzlin' 1958 Buick. The Energeum is operated by the Alberta Energy and Utilities Board. Hours are from 10:30 to 4:30 daily. Call 297-4293 for information.

Stampede founder Guy Weadick was a showman who knew the lasting appeal of the cowboy way of life

Stampede

Nothing about the Calgary Stampede is ordinary. It's big. It's brash. It's fun. Even simple things connected to the Stampede are special. Take the flagpole at Stampede Park. With a Canadian Maple Leaf Flag on top, from a distance, it looks perfectly ordinary.

But it's not. At some 61 metres tall, the flagpole at Stampede Park is the very tallest wooden flagpole in Canada. Officially registered as The Calgary Stampede Flagpole, it is more than four metres taller than the runner-up flagpole at the Canadian National Exhibition in Toronto.

Like the Stampede itself, the Stampede Flagpole is something all Calgarians look up to—since it puts everything else in its shade.

Like many human residents, the flagpole is an oil boom immigrant. It arrived here from Vancouver Island in 1981, just as the finishing touches were being given to that other lanky landmark, the Petro-Canada Tower.

The pole began life as a Douglas fir near Cowichan Lake about 425 years ago and came by train on four railway flatcars. No one counted how many railway workers were required to get it here—nor how concrete finishers worked on the ornamental base built at the South Gate of Stampede Park. However, it is recorded in Stampede archives that 37 loggers worked to convert the tree into a pole. Most of them were employed by British Columbia Forest Products Limited, the lumber company which donated the tree to the citizens of Calgary.

Getting the colossal giant here in one piece was a formi-dable challenge. But then nothing about the Stampede is ever done in half-measures. Considering that the pole contains enough lumber to build one-half of a suburban bungalow, putting the tree to work as a flagpole was an act of charity as well as a technological triumph. After all, it would have been much easier for the 37 loggers to saw the tree up into 2-by-4s and send it to us that way.

Since the first ceremonial flag-raising on June 8, 1982, the Maple Leaf has flown proudly at the top of the pole each summer from May 1 to September 30. The flags used are roughly six metres high and 12 metres wide. The flag has to be replaced every few weeks due to wind and weather damage. In fact, the flagpole crew will go through as many as six flags a year.

The flagpole can be seen poking above the horizon from several kilometres away. It's a glorious sight with the Maple Leaf Flag waving in the summer breeze.

In much the same way, the Stampede itself stands tall above all other social institutions—not just in Calgary, but across Western Canada. In Calgary, there's simply nothing else that involves as many citizens as the Stampede. It's a record unmatched by any other summer fair in Canada. Year after year the Stampede turnstiles click out a total of more than one million visitors. That puts the Stampede in a class by itself, right next to professionally-run theme parks like Disneyland, which operate year-round.

The Stampede is such a dynamic part of Calgary because it has deep roots. It is as natural as the poplar tree and the sacred sweetgrass. The first Stampede was held in Calgary in 1912. At the core of its appeal is the rodeo, where the age-old struggle between man and beast is played out according to rules and customs that have become as formalized as ballet.

The rodeo owes much to the old wild west touring shows, which thrilled audiences around the world in the 19th century. It continues here today because Calgary's pioneer western roots are still very much alive. Despite tremendous change in the cattle industry, for instance, cattlemen still need horses. In other agricultural areas, horses were long ago replaced by trucks and tractors, but the cattle industry guaranteed Calgary would always have cowboys.

Also essential to the Stampede are the native people. The First Nations have been active participants of the Stampede from the very beginning. At first it was one of the few times no one was trying to turn them into imitation white people. The Stampede has been a major influence to help preserve native traditions in Canada. No other city has ever provided such an opportunity to celebrate the traditional native way of life.

From the beginning in 1912, the Stampede built a bridge between cultures. It presented an open invitation to all the native tribes of the region to take a unique leading role in the city's major festival. It brought Calgary city-slickers face-to-face with folks from the country.

Even so, it took a few years for the Stampede idea to really catch on. The years between 1914 and 1918 were taken up by the First World War. Another Stampede was held in 1919, but even then there were many who were unconvinced that it would have lasting appeal.

Finally, in 1923, the

Danny Copithorne, Volunteer

REAL ESTATE EXECUTIVE Danny Copithorne, 62, is past-president of the Stampede Board. He's been a Stampede volunteer since 1968.

I had moved to Edmonton, and I came back in '67. A friend was involved in the Promotion Committee and he said, "You should get involved," so that's exactly all he had to say. The Stampede, back in those days, felt the general public wasn't aware that it was a volunteer not-for-profit organization, so they started the Information Committee. That's how I got involved. We would take along a singer and a piano player. [If] anybody wanted a little bit of entertainment and would give us 20 minutes to talk about the Stampede, why we'd go out and do it.

Being a volunteer becomes a way of life. There's tremendous personal satisfaction, no doubt about that. You get to meet a lot of nice people—I'm talking about the people who work around the Stampede and the people who come in, the ordinary citizens. The best thing is hearing how the city is so well known because of the efforts of the Stampede and because of the efforts of the volunteers and staff. It's been a great experience. I wouldn't trade it for anything.

Stampede was officially linked to the exhibition to form the Calgary Exhibition and Stampede. The citizen-run organization has been part of Calgary's heart and soul ever since.

One way to identify longtime Calgarians is to listen carefully to what they call the place where the Stampede is held. If they call it the Stampede Grounds, you know you're dealing with a genuine old-timer. The proper name these days is Stampede Park, but for decades it was called simply the Grounds, as in, "I'll meet you at the Grounds." Originally, however, the official name was Victoria Park, which was bestowed in the days long before the Stampede was part of the annual exhibition. Slowly, the Victoria Park name was adopted by the nearby residential district.

Rodeo

The rodeo competitions at the Stampede are the ultimate celebration of the wild side of Calgary's western heritage.

Rodeo is strong stuff. It's exotic and plenty dangerous—at least, that certainly is the impression you get after seeing a man get hurled from the back of a rampaging bull. Rodeo looks like a tough way to make a living, and it seems a strange way to have fun. Yet there is plenty of fun (along with a few bruises and generous cash rewards) for rodeo athletes at the Calgary Stampede. For them, it's not strange at all to get tossed in the dirt by a bucking bronc; it's all in a day's work.

Something for everyone on Stampede midway

These riders and ropers and drivers are locked in an entertaining partnership with horses and cattle, the most powerful beasts of the ranch country. At the Stampede, horses and cattle are the royalty of the animal kingdom. They are the most pampered hoofed animals in the world. Many have a working day that's over in eight seconds or less.

Of course, the rodeo is also show biz, but it's show biz with homely traces of manure on its fancy, high-cut boots. Many of the athletes—from bullriders to barrel racers—are genuine farmers and ranchers when they aren't rodeoing. And most of the events they compete in are based on routine ranch chores. Horses must be tamed, wagons hauled, and stray cattle caught. At the Stampede, these com-

mon cowboy skills are polished up and presented as world-class sport.

Rodeo gets in the blood and becomes a family tradition. The same family names keep popping up at the top of the prize lists year after year, decade after decade, generation after generation. It's all in the breeding. Almost every rodeo athlete has a cousin or a

Rodeo is pro sport, and work of art

Cowboys must hold on with one hand only, and are disqualified if they touch the horse with their free hand

grandparent who used to rodeo. In true ranch romance style, some rodeo stars have married and mingled the honored bloodlines to form rodeo dynasties. Rodeo competitors get together after the day. They share expenses and take turns driving the pickup truck to the next rodeo. They become friends for life.

The classic contest between cowboys and cattle, between man and beast, is at the very heart and soul of the Stampede—and has been from the very beginning in 1912. The only difference now is the array of books and computers full of rules and regulations—as well as herds of judges, inspectors, and animal welfare officers—

which govern what happens at the Stampede.

Like other professional sports, rodeo has developed strong links with the business community. Big-name corporations, from auto makers and airlines to banks and breweries, have recognized the value of the clean-cut cowboy image. Companies pay many thousands of dollars for corporate sponsorships and launch major advertising campaigns based on their cowboy connections.

The commercial links, the media involvement, and the competition spurred by increased prize money have helped improve rodeo standards all across Western

Canada and the United States. The athletes have formed professional associations (there's even one for gay cowguys) and travel the circuits from one big show to another, usually dropping in on small-town rodeos along the way. The animals follow the same circuit.

Rodeo athletes come from all over the ranching world—from the US, Australia, and Brazil—to compete at Calgary. The Stampede is known internationally as the fat-purse rodeo. No other rodeo, no state fair, nor any frontier days celebration anywhere can match the Stampede's largesse when it comes to Rodeo's Richest Hour.

The magic hour comes on the final Friday of the infield events. It's a moment of glory that young cowboys dream

Next page: An 8-second ride seems like eternity

Clowns provide rodeo humor

about and that old cowboys remember forever. During Rodeo's Richest Hour, five cowboys are presented with trophies, belt buckles, championship rings, sponsorship bonuses—and Stampede Grand Prize cheques for $50,000 each. It just doesn't get any better.

There are separate sets of rules for each of the five big rodeo sports. Infringements mean additional penalty points that can put a contestant out of the money. There's even a dress code. Anyone who ventures into the infield must be in full western garb, especially the wide-brimmed cowboy hat.

Scoring

A large load of luck helps in the big three riding events: Saddle Bronc, Bareback, and Bull Riding. The rodeo judges base only half the score on a rider's ability; the other half is measured on how well the animal performs. A cowboy who draws a spirited animal will get higher marks. In Saddle Bronc and Bareback, the rider must keep his spurs touching the neck above the horse's shoulders. The spurs are made dull to avoid injuring the animal.

Saddle Bronc

The North American Saddle Bronc Riding Championship held at the Stampede is called a riding event, although there's not much riding involved. A good saddle bronc ride is over in just eight seconds and a bad one is over even sooner. Cowboys are given points for properly spurring the horse while holding onto a small halter with just one hand. The feet must stay in the stirrups, and the free hand must not be used. Cowboys are eliminated if they touch either the horse, the saddle or halter, or themselves with that free hand. The best scores are in the low 90s.

Bareback

It's easy to see how the sport developed from the routines used to train horses to obey a rider's commands. During the North American Bareback

Sonya Dueck, Stampede Queen

U OF C *psychology student Sonya Dueck was Stampede Queen in 1994.*

I think the most important thing I do as Stampede Queen is tell people about Calgary and the people who live in the city and the spirit of the city.

Doing schools is the most fun because kids accept you so unconditionally, and you know you're setting a good example for them, giving them something that's very achievable and something they should be proud of. I also like visiting some of the old folks' homes and lodges because these are some of the people who made the city what it is. I like to hear their stories and how they took part in creating the Stampede and creating Calgary—and being part of Calgary is really special. I've always loved horses, and I've always loved the city of Calgary.

Before I was Queen, I was riding with the Stampede Ranch Girls. They're the girls who carry around the sponsor flags. A lot of those girls were ex-Queens and ex-Princesses, and it showed me how much they wanted to stay involved with the Stampede.

The hard part is some of the long days. I think one of our days at Stampede was 20-some functions, 29 or something, so it was incredibly hard. I mean, it was wonderful too—it's kind of like a happy tired. People keep you going.

A rodeo bucking horse can dispense with its chores in less than 8 seconds

Riding Championship at the Stampede, the lessons last just eight seconds. That way the horses never lose their appetite for bucking. Riders are disqualified for using their free hand to touch themselves, the horse, or the equipment. The best scores are in the high 80s.

Bull Riding

The epitome of the "roughstock" events is the North American Bull Riding Championship at the Stampede. In the infield at all times is a rodeo clown. He looks like a goofy guy, a caricature cowboy, but beneath the rags and silly make-up is a specialist so skilled he has earned the right to call himself a bullfighter. The bullfighter's most important job is to distract the bull in case a tossed rider is in any danger of being trampled or gored. The best scores for Bull Riding are in the low 90s.

Timed Events

A cowboy has to keep the herd together at all times. Any cattle that stray away must be rounded up promptly. The Stampede has taken the all-day job and compressed it into a pair of sports, Calf Roping and Steer Wrestling, that are faster than a basketball breakaway. Both sports are based on the age-old chore of capturing the runaway before it gets to run

Buckles can be works of art

Stampede Facts

Agricultural Society Founded	1884
First Exhibition	1886
First Stampede	1912
Stampede Combined With Exhibition	1923
Young Canadians Debut	1969
Average Attendance ('88-'94)	1.2 million
Stampede Employees (full-time)	240
Stampede Employees (part-time)	1210
Stampede Volunteers	1700

away. In both sports events, the animal has a head-start before the cowboy on horseback is let loose. Starting off too soon results in a punishing 10-second penalty.

Calf Roping

The North American Calf Roping Championship at the Stampede is a test of multiple skills. The cowboy must lasso the calf, dismount, run to the calf, deftly dump it on its side, and tie any three of its legs together. After the calf is tied, the cowboy gets back on his horse and allows the catch line to slacken. If the calf can kick free in six seconds, the cowboy is disqualified. Cowboys are also disqualified if the calf is jerked backwards head over heels during the lassoing. The best ropers can bring in their calf in about seven seconds.

Steer Wrestling

In the same way bull riders receive help from the bullfighter rodeo clowns, the contestants in the North American Steer Wrestling Championship at the Stampede get help from other cowboys in the infield. The assistants are called hazers. The hazers ride on the other side of a running steer and keep it moving in a straight line. Once the steer is let loose, the cowboy chases until he catches up, then swings down off the right side of his horse and grasps the running steer by the horns. He then digs his heels into the soft earth of the infield and attempts to wrestle the steer to the ground in one move. He is allowed to take only one step to catch his balance or get a better grip on the fleeing steer. It must be turned or stopped first and is not considered down until the steer is flat on

Champion bull riders earn their wages one buck at a time

its side or back and all four legs are straight. The best steer wrestlers can complete the task in less than four seconds.

Barrel Racing

The only rodeo sport set aside especially for women is the Calgary Stampede Ladies Barrel Racing Championship. The contestants ride their horses around decorated oil barrels set in a tight cloverleaf pattern. They are timed electronically. It's the ultimate test of a rider's ability to turn quickly and safely. Riders may touch or bump the decorated barrels

but are penalized five seconds for each one they knock down. The best times are less than 17 seconds.

Other Awards

The best athletes at the Calgary Stampede can quickly fill a trophy case at home with various awards. The Guy Weadick Memorial Award, named in memory of the founder of the Stampede, is presented annually to the athlete who makes outstanding accomplishments in rodeo as well as meriting recognition for personality,

A wet day in the infield brings out the best in a cowboy

sportsmanship, and appearance. The Calgary Stampede All-Around Cowboy Championship is awarded to the athlete who has entered at least two of the five major events and who won the most prize money in the first three days of competition.

Next page: The Rangeland Derby!

Isabella Miller, Barrel Racer

ISABELLA MILLER, a former Stampede Princess, is a barrel racer.

Not every horse is going to be a barrel horse. There's some that just don't like it, and if you have to really force them to do it, they're never going to be really good. They have to like it to do it.

It's a slow process, starting the young horse in the training of the barrels because you have to know how much you can give them without making them sour or getting mad. I've usually always managed to have a good horse, and they've all been young

horses. When you can excel with a five-year-old compared to eight, nine, ten and eleven-year-olds,

it's quite an accomplishment, but not all horses can handle that. They have to be very athletic because the running and the turning is very hard on them.

If you can depend a lot on your horse, that makes the whole difference, takes a lot of lead off your back.

Depending on the ground, on a 90 by 110 foot course, it averages from 16.3 seconds up into the 17s. If you knock a barrel down, there's a five second penalty—and going off course, you're disqualified.

Outriders must stay close to their chuckwagons

Chuckwagons

In the early days, the chuckwagon was essential equipment on any ranch. The homely chuckwagon was the pickup truck of the pioneer west. Whenever cowboys rode out to tend the herds, they would toss all their heavy gear into the chuckwagon, including branding irons, maybe a tent or two, and a portable stove for fixing dinner.

Of course, the wagon also carried the chuck, which is what cowboys sometimes call food. (Depending on the skill of the cook, they often call it a lot worse names, but that's another story.)

Chuckwagons first stirred up the dust at the Victory Stampede of 1919, held to celebrate the end of the First World War. The scene was set for excitement. All it needed was something to set it off; all it took was a couple of chuckwagons.

A few cowboys had been cooking up some real rangeland grub for folks attending the Stampede. They had set up their chuckwagons in front of the grandstand. When the time came to pack up, one of the wagon drivers challenged the other to a race.

In a flash they both loaded their wagons, then rumbled

Canvas Cash

PRICE PAID AT auction for advertising space on chuckwagon canvas in 1994:

Driver	Amount
Kelly Sutherland	$80,000
Dallas Dorchester	63,000
Buddy Bensmiller	50,000
George Normand	50,000
Tom Glass	48,000
Jerry Bremner	45,000
Jason Glass	42,000
Hugh Sinclair	40,000
Jim Knight	33,000
Bert Croteau	30,000
Norm Cuthbertson	30,000
Ron David	30,000
Herman Flad	29,000
Doyle Mullaney	29,000
Mike Vigen	27,000
Roy David	25,000
Dennis MacGillvray	25,000
Ward Willard	25,000
Wayne Knight	23,000
Stan Robertson	22,500
Glen Risdale	21,500
Kirk Sutherland	20,500
Brian Laboucane	20,000
Dave Lewis	20,000
Grant Preece	20,000
Edgar Baptiste	19,000
Ray Croteau	19,000
Wayne Dagg	19,000
Ray Mitsuing	19,000
Ed Alstott	18,500
Reg Johnstone	16,500
Ross Knight	16,000
Luke Tournier	14,250
Maynard Metchewals	14,000
Tom Parenteau	14,000
Rod Salmond	11,000

Rodeo competitions are tests of speed and skill

down the racetrack. All the other cowboys jumped up on their horses and joined in. It was a great surprise. The audience loved it.

Stampede organizer Guy Weadick knew a great idea when he saw one. He lined up enough chuckwagons for the next Stampede, held in 1923, to present a spectacular race to end the rodeo competitions each evening.

Ever since, the Rangeland Derby has been a feature of the Stampede. It's part of the bedrock tradition of the Stampede and could be Calgary's only truly unique contribution to the world of sport.

The rules are simple but each race is closely supervised by judges who have absolute discretion to penalize drivers for infractions.

The wagons take their positions in the infield area in front of the grandstand. To give all outfits a fair start, they do a figure-8 loop around strategically-placed barrels, then

Tom Glass, Chuckwagon Champion

HIGH RIVER RANCHER *Tom Glass has won the Stampede Chuckwagon Championship four times.*

It's exciting. Anytime you race it's always exciting, whether you're out front trying to stay there or whether you're behind trying to get to the front. It's always kind of a fun thing.

Getting the inside is pretty important. They figure if you're on the outside of two other wagons, you're probably going to run a full wagon and a horse length further than the guy on the rail. You have to be that much stronger with it.

But then you can back up and get in behind, and if you hang on to your horses and he's letting his run full-out, it's like pacing it on a marathon, pacing it and then coming in at the end. There's lots of jockeying around.

My dad was driving 'em when I was born. My grandfa-

ther drove them before that—my grandfather won the 1924 Stampede. My son Jason is the fourth generation.

I like the excitement of it. I have a lot of friends that are in it, and then they let me win the $50,000 every once in a while. That doesn't hurt my feelings, either.

charge out onto the race track.

Each wagon must have four outriders. At the start of the race, the outriders must toss a stove and tent in the back. The "stoves" are made of rubber, because a real stove would be too dangerous in case of accidents.

There have been a few unfortunate spills on the track over the years, which is why more and more outriders and drivers have taken to wearing helmets.

Today, there is a much higher level of professionalism in chuckwagon racing. Corporations pay thousands of dollars for the privilege of renting the advertising space on the canvas on the back of the wagon. Top drivers follow a circuit of rodeos in Canada and the US.

At the beginning, most of the outriders came from the same ranch as the driver, but soon the best outriders hired themselves out to different drivers on a race-by-race basis. Now, some top outriders will take part in almost every race during an evening at the Stampede, putting on the appropriate colored vest every time they ride on the track.

Teepee Village

When the Stampede hits Calgary, the clock suddenly turns back centuries, and the flats along the Elbow River once again become the scene of a teepee village.

The village is set up on the south end of Stampede Park by the flagpole and includes representatives from all the

First Nations of southern Alberta. Entire families move in from their modern homes on distant reserves and set up their ceremonial teepees.

Then, for the duration of the Stampede, they live as much as possible as their ancestors did. Although it's doubtful that many of those ancestors ever had to put up with such raucous distractions as the noisy midway rides or the late night fireworks.

However, despite the many concessions to modern convenience—

the children who stay at the village will wear running shoes instead of moccasins, for instance—the teepee village and the dance competitions held nearby do offer a glimpse of the ancient traditions of Alberta's native people. During the Stampede, bannock—a tasty piece of edible history— is made at the teepee village.

It is a great honor for native families to participate in the village. When

Designs used to decorate a dancer's regalia often have personal or mystical significance

the Stampede first began, such teepees were still a common sight on the grasslands, but now they are used only for special occasions. They are expensive to make and maintain.

The teepees in the village are decorated with traditional designs that have particular and personal significance for the family owning them. Often a teepee is kept plain until a design is revealed to the owner in a dream; only then is the pattern painted on to the canvas. Each teepee design is unique, and it would be quite improper for anyone to copy the design used by another family.

In similar fashion, the beadwork designs used on dance costumes have special meaning for each dancer. The same holds true for the dance music. Some songs are owned by the drummers and are not to be repeated or copied by others. Most of the drum groups will allow their songs to be tape-recorded by spectators, but some important songs have a particular significance, and recording is forbidden.

Native dancing and dance costumes, like all other aspects of native life, have undergone great changes in recent years. In the same way teepees are now made with canvas instead of buffalo hides, dancers now use modern fabrics and synthetic materials to decorate their costumes.

Dancing at the Stampede and other powwows is often highly competitive. Dancers will spend a great deal of time and money preparing their costumes and practising their steps. Most of the dances stem from a long tradition extending far beyond the first contact with fur traders and pioneer settlers.

Two of the most important dances are the Fancy Dance and the Traditional Dance. Some of the steps used in these dances can be traced back to the story-telling dances linked to men-only warrior societies. Men dancers also participate in the Chicken Dance, which originally was patterned on the fascinating courtship dances of the prairie chicken. The chicken dance classification has changed dramatically in recent years and has led to a new type of dancer, the New Fancy Dancer, which features exceptionally colorful outfits. Some New Fancy Dancers' costumes include shiny mirrors; bright, fluorescent-colored, artificial feathers; and multiple decorated bustles. Even with all the high-tech, shimmering decorations, the dancers maintain the old tradition at the end of the song. Just like a prairie chicken, they freeze in position at the last drum-beat.

At one time, the dance costumes used in the Grass Dance really were made of long woven grasses, but today brightly-colored synthetic yarns are used. Although many of the movements in the Grass Dance are clearly based on hunting manoeuvres, there is also a spiritual component, as if the swaying grass costume was invoking the spirits of the life-giving grasses blowing in prairie breezes.

The most musical of all dancers are the Jingle Dancers, whose costumes are decorated with small bells, often hundreds of them. Some, in fact, will have precisely 365 bells, one for every day of the year. The Jingle Dance is said to have arisen from a medicine woman's vision, and it is assumed to be a health-giving dance. Each jingle of the bells is considered a tiny prayer. A group of Jingle Dancers, dancing together and in unison, softly then more strongly, creates a sound like soft rain or like wind rattling through the branches of tall trees.

7. Southeast

Spend a relaxing day at Fish Creek Park

Apart from a few exceptional residential districts and recreational attractions, the Southeast is Calgary's industrial quadrant. Here are the great factories, the warehouses, and the wholesalers that keep the economy churning. This is where the city's remarkable economic power is put to work. The prime attraction close to the city centre is Stampede Park, where hundreds of thousands of Calgarians go to have fun. It's a year-round centre of activity because there's much more to Stampede Park than the Stampede.

Even if you count the three or four days spent setting up the midway rides, the Greatest Outdoor Show on Earth lasts only a couple of weeks in July. But that doesn't mean Stampede Park sits idle for the remaining 350-odd days. There's something happening somewhere every day of the year.

Within Stampede Park is Calgary's major indoor entertainment venue, the Olympic Saddledome, which is also the home of the Flames Hockey Club. The Saddledome, which has its own administration separate from the Stampede Board, is used for everything from political rallies to concert recitals.

The name for the Saddledome does more than pay homage to Calgary's cowboy heritage, but the roof really does look a lot like a saddle. It is made of interlocking concrete panels which are suspended by steel cables. Remarkably, the unique design of the roof has acoustical benefits. The sound is dispersed so that even the loudest rock bands do not become entirely deafening. Incidentally, one of the little-known charms of the Saddledome is its fine dining room which is much favored by Calgary's movers and shakers. For reservations call 261-0573.

One of the busiest spots in Stampede Park is on the top floor of the Big Four Building. Here is the Stampede Casino, which is operated on behalf of community and charitable groups. The casino dealers and some other workers are paid by the Stampede, but most of the chores involving

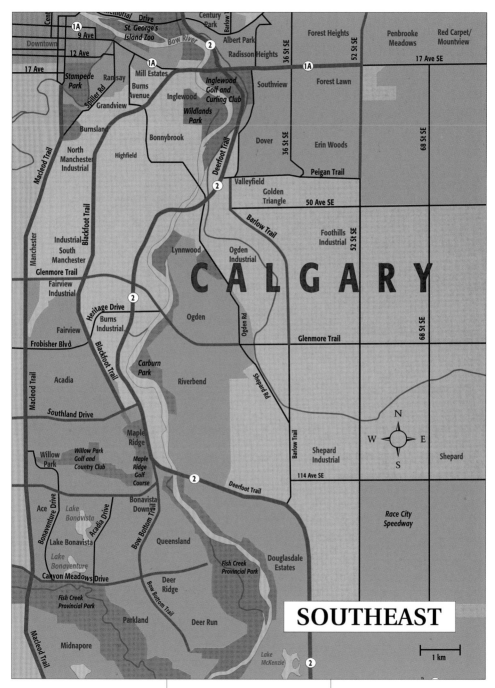

chips and cash, including the counting of the day's proceeds, are done by volunteers from the sponsoring charity.

The Big Four Building was named after the four pioneer cattlemen who were the financial backers of the first Stampede in 1912 — George Lane, Pat Burns, Archie McLean and A.E. Cross.

Horse-racing is a popular

Fish Creek Park is popular year-round playground

attraction at the track. The grandstand building has a well-appointed lounge area and restaurant for track enthusiasts.

The Round-Up Centre is the scene for hundreds of trade shows and exhibitions throughout the year. Most trade shows are restricted to those who work in particular industries or are members of professional associations, but there are many exhibitions that are open to the general public. Among the most popular are shows featuring home renovations, antiques and collectibles.

Stampede Park has a daily events hotline. For current activities call 261-0330.

Fish Creek Park

Canada's largest urban park is Fish Creek Provincial Park in Southeast Calgary. Over 20 kilometres in length and consisting of 1,153 hectares, it is even larger than Nose Hill Park, which has 1,127 hectares.

Fish Creek Park is administered by provincial park wardens. It's a busy place with many separate areas for different activities. Included in the park are areas for swimming, hiking, cycling, hay-rides, picnicking, horse-riding, bird-watching and quietly contemplating nature. There are also important historical buildings from the days of pioneer ranching and settlement. An area along the creek provides nesting sites for a colony of Great Blue Herons. This and another spot with high south-facing cliffs where Prairie Falcons nest are restricted to prevent the rare birds from being disturbed.

Archeologists from the University of Calgary have identified more than 200 prehistoric sites, including animal kill sites and teepee rings. The rings are simple circles of small stones that were used to hold down the sides of teepees. Unfortunately, some of the teepee rings have been tampered with by residents

Southeast Restaurants

RESTAURANT CRITIC John Gilchrist's recommendations for the Southeast:

There is no "restaurant row" in the Southeast. Dining spots are diverse and far-flung.

The Mimo, 4909 - 17th Avenue SE (235-3377) offers excellent Portuguese cuisine. It's an odd setting; you have to walk through the bar to get to the restaurant, but it does have wonderful food.

In the Inglewood district is the **El Inca**, 1325 - 9th Avenue SE (262-7832), which is Calgary's only Peruvian restaurant. It's terrific. Peruvian cuisine is very distinct, using a lot of potatoes and seafood. Chilies are popular ingredients, but this is not really hot Central American cuisine. Discover a very pleasant place.

Also in Inglewood are the **Deane House**, 809 - 9th Avenue SE (269-7747), and the **Cross House**, 1240 - 8th Avenue SE (531-2767), which are historical houses converted into restaurants.

Rather bizarre is Lloyd's Caribbean Bakery. Lloyd, himself, is a hilarious guy. Actually, it's now called **Lloyd's Caribbean Bakery and Bellyful**, 3745 Memorial Drive SE (248-2113). Lloyd has incredible jerk chicken.

from nearby neighborhoods who took the rocks home for their gardens. Visitors are reminded not to remove anything from the park.

Calgary's riverbank trail system is one of the best ways to see Fish Creek Park, either on foot or on bicycle. The park wardens and a dedicated corps of citizen volunteers present a variety of programs to make a visit to the park more enjoyable and educational. Small study kits are available to help visitors identify trees, birds and other animals who make their home in the park. For further information call 297-5293.

Midnapore

Just whisper the name "Midnapore" and you've got yourself a sure-fire way to tell a genuine old-time Calgarian from a newcomer of similar age. To anyone who's been in Calgary for only a decade or two, Midnapore is the location of attractive suburban developments on the city's south side.

But to Calgarians who can look back to the 1950s or earlier, the very idea that Calgary swallowed Midnapore in one gulp is conclusive proof that Calgary Has Grown Too Big.

Midnapore used to be a village and was established in 1883. For pioneer Calgarians, it was a big excursion to drive as far as Midnapore. There were places for picnics out that way, especially along the banks of Fish Creek.

In those days, there were great expanses of wide-open prairie between Midnapore and its encroaching neighbor. It was annexed in 1961 and, in recent years, has even been passed by newer subdivisions marching flat out all the way to Okotoks, Priddis, and beyond.

Midnapore still has traces of its ancient village background. There are a few old houses and well-preserved pioneer churches, especially the old St. Paul's Anglican Church, which has a cemetery with headstones dating back as far as 1886.

Bernard Callebaut

BERNARD CALLEBAUT came to Calgary 12 years ago from Belgium, where his family had been making chocolates for four generations. Today more than two dozen shops across Canada and the US are selling the candies made in Calgary at 1313 - 1st Street SE.

One of the reasons I came to Calgary was the entrepreneur spirit. Calgary is definitely an entrepreneur city. People take risks. They try things. I like that. Also, in the long term, I believe Alberta is a province with tremendous potential because we have all these natural resources. A country like Belgium doesn't have anything. Combine that with the mountains, that's what I like.

And the people here, they are very dedicated. We have a good working force here. In the Christmas season, we worked basically 13 Saturdays. People came and did their job. Business is good, it's good for them too. There's a good mentality here, but I found that out later. I didn't know when I came.

I never doubted the product. The demand always grew bigger and bigger. Once I saw the initial reaction, I knew there was a market. It's the same now in the US We've just opened the first shop in the US at Kirkland, Washington, just east of Seattle. It looks very promising. The response of the people was fantastic. We're starting there from scratch again. Nobody knows us, and the reaction is good. So if we fail, it's a mistake on the management side. It's not the product.

Only three stores are head-office owned. The rest are dealerships. At the head office we have a strip mall. We're going to lease out the spaces to complementary businesses, but most of the building we're going to use.

At the head office people can view the manufacturing. There is a hallway we built for the purpose. It has windows so people can watch. It's open from Monday to Friday from 10 to 5.

Zoo

CALGARY'S ZOO IS one of the city's great treasures. It's much more than a zoo. For that matter, as its proper name indicates, it's the Calgary Zoo, Botanical Garden and Prehistoric Park. Most certainly, the zoo is a celebration of both plant and animal life from the beginning of time.

Here Calgarians are able to stroll through a tropical rain forest even in the depths of winter. They see eagles and elephants, beavers and butterflies, even tigers and tulips. It's a wonderful place, one of the finest nature spaces on the continent.

The zoo began in the middle of the Bow River on St. George's Island, which has been one of Calgary's most popular recreational areas since it was first developed as a park in 1912. Putting a few pens for animals on the island was something of an afterthought. In 1917 two mule deer were captured within the city, and there was no other place to take them. They became an instant attraction.

In 1920 city council spent $13.04 to build better pens for the deer and a pool display for a pair of turtles someone had donated. Other donations included a kangaroo and a swan from the city clerk, and a black-tail deer from a traveling roadshow, the Johnny Jones Circus. Calgary Zoo was still very small but was the most popular part of the park.

It wasn't until 1929, however, that the zoo really got going. In January, a Zoological Society was formed and was immediately put to a test. The Bow flooded the island in June, and the animals had to be rescued. Then, on October

Prehistoric park features giants from the past

4, Tom Baines was hired by the city to be a combination zookeeper and gardener. He got the job just in time. The stock market crashed later that month; Baines was the last city worker hired for almost a decade.

Tom Baines dedicated his life to the zoo. During the Depression of the '30s, he rode a bicycle to local stores to get food scraps for the animals. Eventually in 1964, he retired as Zoo Director but he continued to work as a zoo volunteer until his health failed. He died in 1994. The bridge at the northwest end of the island is named in his honor.

The Zoological Society has at-tracted many of Calgary's most energetic and generous citizens. The late Eric Harvie, who also started both the Glenbow Museum and Heritage Park, donated

Zoo Facts

Open	365 days a year
Number of animal exhibits	1,240
Annual attendance	785,000
Information line	232-9372

Ample parking space, even for RVs and buses, is available at the Main Entrance of the Zoo along Memorial Drive NE.

Zoo

Zoos trade animals to prevent inbreeding

squeeze onto the island. Now, instead of living in apartment-sized cages, animals are allowed to roam in enclosures that resemble their natural habitat as much as possible.

On the north side of the Bow River, the zoo has the Prehistoric Park, which has lifelike dinosaur models shown in a natural setting. As well, there is the Canadian Wilds, a re-creation of important habitat types found in Canada. When completed, the Canadian Wilds will be the largest natural habitat display of native plants and animals in the country.

many animal exhibits, including giraffes and rare white rhinos, as well as the conservatory.

From the very beginning, St. George's Island has been a horticultural showplace. It started as little more than a scruffy gravel bar, so gardeners had to work hard to improve the soil. Today, thanks to the conservatory, it is a year-round garden.

The first dinosaurs at Calgary Zoo were built during the 1930s. The largest and most famous is Dinny, but the most accurate dinosaur models are in the Prehistoric Park where they are set up amid plants resembling the greenery that the real dinosaurs either ate or in which they hid.

In recent years the zoo has taken on a new mandate to ensure endangered species don't follow the dinosaurs into extinction. Animals are traded with other zoos to prevent inbreeding and to ensure the survival of gorillas and other species from countries where the natural habitats have disappeared.

Originally, Calgary Zoo was packed with as many different species as the zookeepers could

The ostrich cannot fly, but is a very fast runner

Big Rock Brewery

AS FAR AS the gourmets of beer are concerned, there is only one Michael Jackson worth listening to. Unlike his namesake in the entertainment industry, the beer critic Michael Jackson is an author, not a pop singer. He is best known for his book, *The World Guide to Beer*, and is renowned for his sober judgment on the heady subject.

When Jackson first scrutinized a Big Rock beer, he declared it to be "the most distinctive beer in Canada." He praised Big Rock's strongest brew, McNally's Extra Ale, as the best of its type in the

tering holes as far away as California and Colorado.

Big Rock is on a roll. It has succeeded in hewing out a comfortable niche market in a field dominated by monster, multi-national brewing companies. The big companies, using saturation advertising campaigns, regularly soak up almost the entire market, leaving only one or two per cent of production to slop over to the smaller labels. Big Rock is now classed among the top five regional breweries on the continent and has

distinctive taste. The gap in the market was small but clear to McNally. He was no stranger to the business. He was a lawyer, and he owned a farm on which he raised barley. He also liked a good glass of beer and wondered how the big breweries could take the finest Alberta barley and turn it into such an undistinguished product.

"There was nobody brewing beer," McNally explains. "It's a matter of definition. I say there was no beer available. There was beer that was maybe 40 to

world. "McNally's Extra Ale may be Canadian," he said, "but it is the best Irish-style ale I have ever tasted."

Big Rock Brewery Ltd. began small in 1985. Compared to the battling giants of the brewing industry, it's still small, just a speck of foam on an ocean of beer. But Big Rock is riding high on a wave of local popularity and is now making a splash in selected wa-

beer on sale across most of the western half of Canada and the US. The company has gone public and is listed on the Alberta Stock Exchange and NASDAQ.

As Jackson noted, Big Rock is great beer. Ed McNally, Big Rock's founding president, saw there was room for a quality brew that could be sold as a high-end, luxury beverage. Using new filtering technology to do away with the need for pasteurization, he was able to make beers retaining their

45 per cent beer, but I don't think that's beer. What we wanted to make was beer, correct, fully 100 per cent beer. That was the simplistic attitude we had at the start."

McNally's attitude on marketing was just as simple. He had no money for advertising, so he gave people something to talk about by giving his company and his beers a series of unusual names. In Calgary, Big Rock already meant something. It referred to the massive boulder

Big Rock Brewery

Ed McNally with one of the Big Rock family

near Okotoks, left by a retreating glacier during the last ice age. The Big Rock name had solid appeal even before the first batch of beer was brewed. Then came the strange and saucy names for particular brews: Cock o' The Rock Porter, Cold Cock Winter Porter, Warthog Ale, Grasshopper Wheat Ale, and the newest brew, Magpie Rye Ale.

Big Rock put its beers in bottles and boxes designed to make it a special experience to open up a Big Rock. Instead of the common aluminum cans or twist-top bottles, Big Rock has remained with the traditional beer bottle requiring an old-fashioned bottle opener.

In the same way, the compa-

ny has strayed far from the usual paths in presenting its products. Most brewers are battling for the sports market. Big Rock has gone for the arts and is more likely to advertise on a program for a ballet than one for a ball game.

Much of the Big Rock image is the creation of Dirk Van Wyk, the artist responsible for the company's labels and package design.

Van Wyk, a freelance artist who also teaches occasional courses at the U of C and elsewhere, sees his work for Big Rock as the strongest possible alliance between business and the arts. "The relationship with business intrigues me," he says. "I think that a lot of times the idea of business supporting the arts as a

separate thing just encourages alienation of the arts. Integration of the arts with industry is the only solution towards the good life."

Van Wyk's label designs are quixotic works of art. He likes to play tricks, like leaving out the crossbar of the A on the Pale Ale label or tipping the world on its side for Grasshopper. The images are memorable.

"Well, you know," says McNally, "we didn't advertise, so we wanted our beer to appear different. Our beer sort of demands an original appearance. We wanted our beer to be identified properly, and I think Dirk's calligraphy and art went a long way to doing that."

8. Southwest

Some of Calgary's most attractive neighborhoods are built along the Elbow Valley, from Elbow Park to the luxury neighborhoods encircling Glenmore Park

Calgarians are never satisfied. They're always changing things. Everything is on the move all the time. The city's Southwest is where that restless spirit is most dominant. It's the fickle district where fashion is king. Just the other day it seemed that the city's hottest spot for evening entertainment was a one-block strip of 11th Avenue between 5th and 6th Streets SW. Things got so exciting in the popular nightspots there, folks started calling the area Electric Avenue. On warm summer evenings, so many young fun-seekers wandering around meant that traffic would be stopped.

The high-voltage nickname is still used, but lately the old spark has dimmed along Electric Avenue. Nightclubs have closed as a result of the power failure, leaving only a warm lingering glow in the ones that remain.

The hot Southwest evening scene is always in motion. Many of the party people have jumped even further south to 17th Avenue, but some hopped over to 12th Avenue, and others took a long hike back to the 4th Street scene. There's a wide range of nightspots, from raucous rock to refined retro. Fashion isn't just king in the Southwest. It's also queen. Calgary's flourishing gay clubs, some of which hold drag nights, are virtually all in the Southwest between 10th and 17th.

Even sober-minded real estate developers are swinging with the fashions in the Southwest. Buildings that once were staid offices and warehouses are now being transformed into trendy, loft-style apartments. The shift in use is bringing a new kind of nightlife to some Southwest streets. The scene is calmer, with the emphasis on cappuccino rather than cocktails.

For most of the century, the Southwest has been the preferred address for Calgary's social elite. The trend was established when the CPR's real estate developers planned the Mount Royal district. Building lots were made larger than elsewhere, and permanent restrictions were put on title deeds to protect property

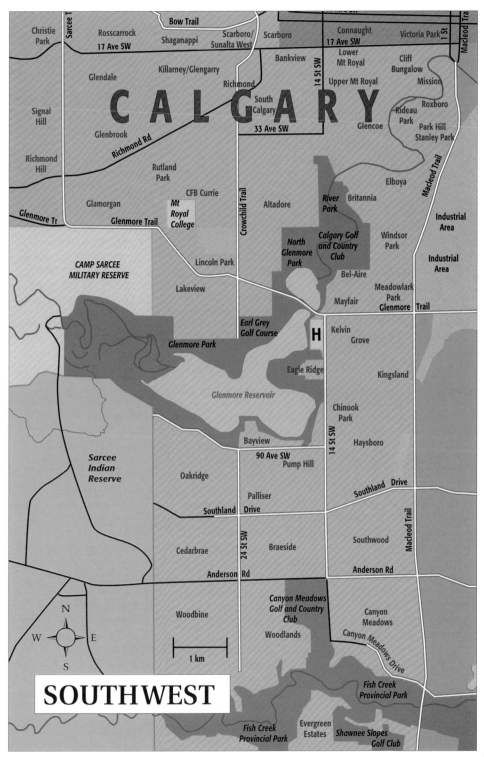

SOUTHWEST

values. The district immediately became the haven of the wealthy and the well-to-do. Mount Royal was the first golden link in a long chain of pricey, residential districts that stretched further and further into the southwest hills along the banks of the Elbow River and along Elbow Drive. With very few exceptions, the Southwest retained fashionable leadership until the 1960s and '70s, when elegant, residential districts were built in the hills by the university in the Northwest, and around artificial lakes in the far Southeast.

Elbow River

Calgarians are so used to the Elbow River no one ever seems to notice that it has a strange name.

Elbow? Why Elbow? The answer runs deep into Calgary's past. The name is a living link with the native tribes who had a habit of naming geographical features after things close at hand, especially body parts. Nose Hill is the other prime local example, but elsewhere in Alberta are Hand Hills, Knee Hill and Belly River. The Elbow probably got its name because of its sharp, elbow-shaped bends, especially the abrupt right-angled bend that wraps around Stampede Park. The Elbow Valley bottomlands had been a popular native camping area for hundreds of years.

Early settlers had fun with the Elbow's bizarre but beautiful name. One prominent and prosperous pioneer family, the Jephsons, had a very large house on the riverbank. Even so, the Jephsons made their friends chuckle when they said in mock distress, "Oh, we're out at Elbow," as if they were in poverty and had to wear clothes with holes in the sleeves.

In pioneer days, the Elbow River was a distant destination for many Calgarians. The earliest settlement in the Southwest was the Mission district south of 17th Avenue between 4th Street and the riverbank. Mission got its name because it was, in fact, the site of a small, log church built by Catholic missionaries.

The humble building was the beginning of the Catholic presence in Calgary. Today, just a few blocks away from that site are the St. Mary's Cathedral and other important church buildings.

Further upstream, the Elbow River had another name.

Southwest Restaurants

RESTAURANT CRITIC John Gilchrist's recommendations for the Southwest:

First of all, there's the major league 4th Street row of restaurants offering probably the best dining in a close vicinity within the city. You will discover the **Da Paolo Ristorante**, 510 - 17th Avenue SW (228-5556), at the north end. Da Paolo's is elegant Italian cuisine, very traditional but very good. At the other end, you have the **Latin Corner**, 2004 - 4th Street SW (244-0033), which is Venezualan and serves the food of South America in an old Dairy Queen—lovely, bizarre setting; great people; and excellent reasonably-priced food.

Across the street is **Jennifer's Jamaican Cuisine**, 2015 - 4th Street SW (228-6966), for Calgary's best Jamaican cuisine—a real fun kind of place to enjoy the warmth of the Caribbean.

The anchor of 4th Street is **4th Street Rose**, 2116 - 4th Street SW (228-5377), which is a California deli-type cafe—always pretty good food, reasonable prices, interesting setting.

Nearby is the **Rajdoot**, 2424 - 4th Street SW (245-0181), which is Calgary's best Indian food, Punjabi-style. Certainly, the curries are excellent.

On 17th Avenue, there's the **Sultan's Tent**, 909 - 17th Avenue SW (244-2333), for Moroccan cuisine. It's excellent.

Restaurant Indonesia, 1604 - 14th Street SW (244-0645), again shows the Asian influence—a great setting and fabulous food. The satays are wonderful.

Entre Nous, 2206 - 4th Street SW (228-5525), is one of our inviting French bistros. The other in the Southwest is the **Jojo Bistro Parisienne**, 917 - 17th Avenue SW (245-2382).

The best new restaurant in the city, as I've so humbly proclaimed, is **Florentine**, 1014 - 8th Street SW (232-6028). It has wonderful, contemporary, Mediterranean cuisine with desserts that actually taste as good as they look.

Mescalero, 1315 - 1st Street SW (266-3339), has intriguing burnt-out decor with southwestern cuisine. For sushi, **Kyoto 17**, 908 - 17th Avenue SW (245-3188), is good and very pleasant.

It was sometimes called the Swift River. In pioneer days the Elbow truly was swift. Today, except for exceptionally rainy summers, the Elbow is a slowly-moving stream within city limits. The reason is simple. Calgarians keep drinking it up. Once the Elbow flows out of the foothills into Calgary, it is captured by the water treatment plant at the Glenmore reservoir. From there the water is piped to the southern half of the city. The

Coste House

COSTE HOUSE IS just another private house today, a very large and elegant private house, mind you, but just another house.

Yet for more than a dozen years the grand mansion in the Mount Royal district was the very heart and soul of Calgary's cultural community. As the Calgary Allied Arts Centre, the house was the home of virtually every artistic enterprise in town.

Coste House was Calgary's premier public art gallery. The big front room was a concert hall for string quartets and solo performers. There was an etching press in the basement, and a room was set aside upstairs for weaving. The old library was used as a cinema for the first season of the Calgary Film Society, which became the largest film society in Canada.

Actors came to Coste House to rehearse. Children came for art lessons. Young dancers came to learn ballet. Young and old alike came to hear Bob Kerr play records from his personal collection at music appreciation sessions. Kerr, of course, went on to become one of Canada's most renowned radio announcers as host of the CBC Stereo show *Off the Record*.

Even the cramped attic space under the rambling roof was put to work. It was taken over by model railroad fanciers who filled the room with scale-model mountains and other miniature backdrops for their tiny trains.

Coste House was once the hub of Calgary's cultural community

Coste House was built as the home of Eugene Coste, a prominent pioneer of the oil and gas industry. It was taken over by the city during the Depression in default of taxes. During the Second World War, the house was used as an art school, which later became the Alberta College of Art.

In 1946, some city aldermen wanted to tear the house down and sell off the six lots that the house occupied. But the Calgary Allied Arts Council convinced them to rent the house for one dollar a year. A former newspaper editor, Archie Key, was hired as director. Key was very definitely the key player at Coste House. At the beginning, he even lived in the old servants' quarters.

The Calgary Allied Arts Centre was a grand success. Similar community arts centres were set up across Canada and the US.

However, as the city got larger, the Centre outgrew the house. There wasn't enough parking outside and not enough space indoors.

So in 1959, Coste House was sold and became a private residence. The Centre moved downtown to a former warehouse. The success continued there for less than a decade. Key retired as director in 1964. In 1969, the Centre went bankrupt.

It left a great gap, one not filled until years later with the opening of the Glenbow Museum and the Calgary Centre for Performing Arts.

Heritage Park

HERITAGE PARK is Calgary's time machine.

On 66 of the prettiest acres under heaven, Calgarians can stroll through history, from the distant days of the fur trade up to the time of the First World War. This time machine really works. Heritage Park has all the sights, the sounds, and even some of the sweetest smells of the genuine old west.

The park is on a hillside with commanding views of Glenmore Lake and the Rockies beyond. It's a dream landscape—gardened and groomed to perfection but still looking as natural as can be.

It's a glorious place to be on a sunny day, but Heritage Park is even more evocative on a rainy afternoon. Foul weather keeps the crowds away, which makes the place look even more authentic. So come anyway. There are plenty of places to get warm.

The good old days of yesteryear come to life. Historic houses sit picture-perfect against a backdrop of poplars. A horse-drawn wagon pauses patiently at a railway crossing as a puffing train rattles past. At the lakeshore, a stern-wheel riverboat toots its whistle as it prepares to depart.

Heritage Park is Canada's largest historical village and attracts 25,000 visitors annually. Opened in 1964 and constantly growing, it is now a polished showcase for more than 100 buildings. More than 70 are originals and look the way they did the day

Steam trains were the chief means of transportation for early settlers

they were built. The rest are newly-built replicas of old-style buildings.

All the original buildings were brought to the park after being saved from demolition in Calgary or outlying towns. They include some of the earliest structures built in Western Canada, including the 1883 house of Sam Livingston, one of Calgary's first settlers. Many

of the houses were rescued from downtown districts being overrun by high-rise office towers during the 1960s and '70s. The three-storey, brick Prince House, the Park's most elegant mansion, was moved in sections from its former site in the downtown Eau Claire district. Moving and rebuilding expenses were paid by the gas company which wanted to build on the property.

Other buildings came from remote towns and rural areas. Residents of Millarville come to visit their much-loved 1895 Ranchers' Hall. Farmers from central Alberta are charmed by the picturesque 1920 windmill that once graced a farm near Bruderheim. Folks from Canmore make a pilgrimage to the park to see their cozy 1898 log Opera House. There is power in the Opera House logs. The rustic theatre was the birthplace of Alberta Theatre Projects. The theatre troupe outgrew the park and now is resident company at the

Heritage Park

Historic buildings were rescued from surrounding towns and villages

Martha Cohen Theatre in the Calgary Centre for Performing Arts.

An expedition to the pioneer past starts long before visitors approach the front gate. An antique streetcar, just like the sparkwagons that ran on Calgary streets from 1909 until 1950, delivers visitors from the parking lot to the entrance. The streetcar conductor wears an authentic uniform. Everyone working at the park always dresses in vintage style.

Always wave to the engineer!

Heritage Park is administered for the city by the Heritage Park Society, which was founded in 1963. Calgary's great philanthropist, the late Eric Harvie, provided major financial support and inspired dozens of other backers to join in, from large corporations to service clubs. As well, Harvie contributed literally thousands of historic artifacts his Glenbow Foundation had gathered, including artworks, house furnishings, farm equipment, store fixtures, and countless other artifacts of daily life from days gone by. Characteristically, Harvie sought little thanks for his efforts and made most of his contributions quietly through charitable agencies.

One of Heritage Park's most romantic attractions is the Moyie, a scaled-down version of the paddlewheel riverboats which once navigated the lakes and rivers of Western Canada. The Moyie is named after the last boat in the West to be retired from active service, now on display at Kaslo, BC. Heritage Park's Moyie was built at Vancouver, tested in the coastal waters, then dismantled and sent to Calgary by rail. After the ship was re-assembled and officially certified, it sailed its maiden voyage on Glenmore reservoir on August 21, 1965.

The park's railway attracts steam-train enthusiasts from all over the world. Park admission includes a free ride on the train, which tours through all areas of the park as it completes its circuit.

Buildings in the park are arranged according to appropriate historical periods. The fur trading fort and the farm houses are set apart from the town.

The most popular area for children is the historic amusement area, featuring a selection of restored carnival rides. Parents will appreciate the nearby Eugene Coste Park, which is set up like the formal civic gardens once decorating towns across the West.

Park Facts

HERITAGE PARK DEBUTED on Canada's birthday, July 1, 1964.

Visitors are welcome daily from the Victoria Day (May 24th) weekend until Labor Day. At other times it is open on weekends for special events and is available for private functions.

The park is located at 1900 Heritage Drive SW. Call 259-1900 for information.

north, of course, is served by the Bow.

The reservoir is Calgary's largest body of water, and it is the centrepiece of Glenmore Park, one of the finest recreational areas in the city. Swimming is prohibited and so are motorboats; but canoes, kayaks, and small sailboats are allowed. Except for rescue boats and other official watercraft, there is only one big exception to the no-motor rule. It is the Moyie, the picturesque, paddle-wheel riverboat operated by Heritage Park. On a sunny summer's day, when the Moyie splashes by an armada of sailboats, there is not a prettier sight in the whole wide world.

Naval Museum

High on a hill overlooking downtown Calgary, many hundreds of kilometres from the nearest ocean, is the second-largest naval

museum in Canada.

The Naval Museum of Alberta honors the men and women from the prairie provinces who answered the call of the sea since the Royal Canadian Navy was established in 1910. It is officially dedicated to the memory of Lt. Robert Hampton Gray, VC, DSC, RCNVR, the only member of the Royal Canadian Navy in the Second World War to be awarded the Victoria Cross. Gray was born in BC but enlisted at HMCS Tecumseh.

The museum began humbly with a very small but precious collection of just three vintage "warbirds," fighter airplanes that had flown from the decks of Canadian aircraft carriers. The planes

had been on display for many years in front of the headquarters of HMCS Tecumseh. A group of volunteers launched the Tecumseh Historical Society in 1984, with a

Calgary's first public library is a registered landmark and has a popular art gallery on the top floor

mandate to move the rare aircraft indoors to protect them from damage caused by the weather.

Very quickly the society gathered a vast hoard of other naval artifacts, ranging from small identification badges to huge, scale models of some of Canada's most famous fighting ships. Historic photographs show sailors at work—and at play.

One of the rarest displays is an Ogden Gun, a weapon manufactured in Calgary during the Second World War at the Ogden Shops of the Canadian Pacific Railway. Only 1,001 Ogden Guns were made, and most were broken up for scrap after the war. The three-inch, 12-pound weapons were mounted on minesweepers and frigate-class vessels, as well as some merchant ships.

For many visitors, however, the star exhibits will always be the three airplanes, although there will always be differences of opinion about the virtues of each type. The Supermarine Seafire Mk. XV was the sea-going version of the better-known Spitfire. The

Hawker Sea Fury Mk. II was the fastest piston-powered aircraft ever commissioned and was able to out-manoeuvre early jet fighters. The museum's McDonnell Banshee F2H-3 jet has served under two flags. It was in the US Navy before it was acquired by the Royal Canadian Navy.

The museum is on the grounds at the HMCS Tecumseh base at the corner of 17th

Avenue and 24th Street SW. It is open Tuesday to Friday from 1 to 5 pm each afternoon and from 10 am to 6 pm on weekends. Admission is free but donations are welcomed. Call 242-0002 for information.

Military Museum

Calgary's long tradition of military service is commemorated at the Museum of the Regiments, which is the largest

Nellie McClung

FOR A FEW years in the mid-1920s to the early '30s, Nellie McClung was one of Calgary's most famous women. The feminist politician and author of 17 novels and volumes of short stories had a home in Southwest Calgary at 803 - 15th Avenue SW. McClung was elected to the provincial legislature and was one of the Famous Five who led the legal struggle to have women accepted as persons under Canadian law. She moved to Victoria in 1932.

First Settlers

CALGARY'S VERY FIRST settlers, John Glenn and Sam Livingston, had traveled the world before they built their final homes in Calgary. Both were born in Ireland in the 1830s, and both had spent many years rambling across North America.

They were good men of high principle. Glenn was drafted by the rebels in Texas during the US Civil War, but he loathed slavery, so he deserted and joined the Union side. And Livingston refused to stock alcohol at his trading post in the Springbank area west of Calgary. He was one of the first to urge the Mounties to bring law and order to the foothills.

They found their Métis wives in the West. Glenn married Ade-

Sam Livingston

laide Belcourt, and Livingston wed Jane Mary Howse. By the fall of 1973, John and Adelaide were honeymooning in a cabin where Fish Creek joins the Bow. A few months later Sam and Jane became neighbors; the Livingston farm was in the Elbow valley and is now beneath the Glenmore reservoir.

The Glenns and Livingstons prospered. The CPR bought their grain and vegetables to show the world how fertile the West was. The Glenns created the first irrigation project in Western Canada. The Livingstons imported the first fruit trees.

Sam died peacefully in 1897, but John died prematurely in 1886 after being brutally beaten in a fight over some horses.

Reservoir Bogs

Weaselhead area gives many Calgarians a close-up look at nature

CALGARIANS FORGET ALL about Calgary when they go to the Weaselhead.

The sound of traffic and other urban annoyances fade away. There is little to indicate a big city is nearby. Some paths are paved, and there are few fences and signs to remind visitors not to stray onto hillsides that have suffered erosion through excessive traffic. Apart from this, the Weaselhead looks pretty much the way it did centuries ago.

The Weaselhead is at the western end of the Glenmore reservoir in Southwest Calgary. The area is one of Calgary's richest natural habitats. It includes sections of poplar and spruce forest, shrubby meadows, as well as extensive wetlands. It is the home of frogs and chipmunks; sparrows, hawks and owls; as well as deer and the occasional coyote.

The area is named after a respected elder of the Tsuu T'Ina Nation who lived and hunted upstream in the Elbow Valley. The reserve lands of the Tsuu T'Ina are directly to the west.

Through the Weaselhead, there is an extensive pathway system based on old roads, former river channels, and hiking trails. Bicycles are allowed, but motor vehicles are not permitted. Parking lots are plentiful in nearby Glenmore Park; the most convenient lot is just west of the Park's 37th Street entrance.

The Weaselhead is prime territory for birdwatchers. The river and reservoir combine to create a variety of nesting spots, changing through the year as the reservoir water level fluctuates. Migrating species use the sloughs and mudflats as stopover points in the spring and fall. Some birders have even set up birdfeeders along the main pathways to make sure their feathered friends never go hungry.

Calgarians who love nature have strong feelings for the Weaselhead. City traffic planners proposed putting a freeway through the area, but many voices were raised against the plan. The debate continues, but it seems the public mood has shifted in favor of keeping the Weaselhead the way it is.

The colorful life of the cowboy lies at the heart of Calgary's past

military museum in Western Canada and was opened by the Queen in 1990.

The four major regiments in which Calgarians have served are all represented: Lord Strathcona's Horse (Royal Canadians), Princess Patricia's Canadian Light Infantry, King's Own Calgary Regiment, and Calgary Highlanders. The Straths and the PPCLI are both active regiments but the King's Own and the Highlanders are now militia units.

The displays at the museum include lifelike portrayals of Calgary troops in action—fighting from house to house in Europe during the Second World War or on horseback during the Boer War in Africa. A vast array of audio-visual equipment has been installed to provide the sights and sounds of combat. Scale models of famous battlefields have been assembled to explain battle strategies.

The memorabilia includes weapons captured from enemy soldiers as well as handmade artifacts collected by Calgarians who were prisoners of war. There are exhibits of medals won in the heat of battle as well as gifts of appreciation from towns liberated by Calgary troops.

To demonstrate that the tradition of military service continues to this day, the museum also has regularly-updated displays showing the very latest accomplishments by Calgarians who are participating in various United Nations peace-keeping assignments around the world.

It is located near what has been the Canadian Forces Base Calgary, 4520 Crowchild Trail SW. The entrance is located off Flanders Road. The museum is open every day except Wednesday from 10 am to 4 pm. Call 240-7057 for information. Admission is free but donations are welcomed.

Tsuu T'Ina

WHEN ANDERSON ROAD rolls west across 37th Street SW, it becomes the main entrance of the Tsuu T'Ina Nation (formerly the Sarcee Indian reserve). Known to Ottawa bureaucrats as Indian Reserve No. 145, the Tsuu T'Ina Nation is one of the most successful in Canada. Tsuu T'Ina, by the way, is pronounced "sut inna" to rhyme with "put inna".

There are about 1,000 members of the Tsuu T'Ina Nation. Their most conspicuous success is the Redwood Meadows golf course and real estate development at the Bragg Creek end of their land. The golf course provides jobs and cash flow, and the leased lots in the residential development put to use scenic land that had marginal potential for agriculture.

The real showpiece, however, is the new administration centre, built to resemble a beaver dam — a symbol of great importance to the Tsuu T'Ina. Tribal elders trace their roots to the Beaver Clan of the Dene people, who now are based in the Yukon and Northwest Territories. Another branch moved south and became the Apache and Navajo tribes in the US.

The old name, Sarcee, was given to them by other native tribes. In 1991, the band council officially adopted their original name. In Athapaskan, Tsuu T'Ina has layers of meaning including "water people," "beaver people," or "a great number of people." Tribal members had always used the name among themselves.

The Tsuu T'Ina have their own schools. They own natural gas wells, gravel pits, a service station and automobile repair garage, a convenience store, a cattle company, and a construction firm. As well, they have their own herd of buffalo.

The Nation has an economic development commission and has plans to create a second golf course which likely will be called Buffalo Run.

The Tsuu T'Ina land is exceptionally scenic but is private and no trespassing is allowed. However, guided tours are available by calling 281-3363. There is a museum as well; for details call 238-2677.

Spruce Meadows

AT SPRUCE MEADOWS, one Calgary family's fanatical love affair with horses has been transformed from a private passion into a public attraction of international reputation.

Spruce Meadows events attract more then 300,000 visitors annually. Television networks broadcast programs from its media centre to more than 25 nations with a global audience of more than 100 million viewers. Thanks to financial support from major corporations, Spruce Meadows competitions are able to offer the world's top prize money for show jumping.

This phenomenal facility all began as a pleasant family hobby for Marg and Ron Southern and their daughters, Nancy and Linda. The saga of the Southerns is one of Calgary's happiest success stories. It began in 1946 when Ron's father, the late Don Southern, started a modest backyard business making trailers. The Alberta Trailer Company (ATCO) grew quickly through the 1950s since it made trailers that could be used as portable offices and bunkhouses by the booming oil industry. Eventually the trailer division was sold, but by then the family company had branched out into other sectors and now has a commanding position in the marketing of natural gas and electric power.

That financial success made it possible for the Southerns to build Spruce Meadows the way they wanted it, without compromise. They selected a site on the distant southwest outskirts of Calgary, and there they created one of the finest equestrian centres on the planet. The city has since grown almost to the centre's front gate, but it's still outside city limits, even though it has a Calgary street address: 18011 - 14th Street SW. To get there, take Macleod Trail South, turn west at Highway 22X, and follow the signs.

Construction work began at Spruce Meadows in 1973. The facility officially opened in 1975 and held its first tournament in 1976. While Spruce Meadows has grown, the family keeps a close rein on it. Linda Southern-Heathcott is now the leader of Team Spruce Meadows, which competes in a variety of events each year. Linda is also a member of Team Canada, as was her older sister Nancy a decade or so ago.

Spruce Meadows is a virtual village unto itself. There are more than 20 buildings, including seven stables, an indoor Riding Hall, a three-storey Tournament Centre, the Congress Hall, media centre, and sundry maintenance and storage barns. It covers 315 acres, of which about half is used for pasture, hay, or parking during events. Full-time staff total around 70, and as many as 500 volunteers are called on to help during show competitions.

Show jumping is the major public attraction, but Spruce Meadows is the capital of equestrian activity in Western Canada in many more ways. The stable has become renowned as the home of a prize-winning breeding herd of Hanoverians.

The professional approach has put Spruce Meadows on the map wherever equestrian sports are appreciated. The facility has been honored by a visit in 1990 by the Queen, who initiated the Queen Elizabeth II Cup. The tulip growers of Holland have acknowledged Spruce Meadows by naming a hybrid tulip bulb after it. More than 10,000 tulip bulbs blossom each spring in the gardens at Spruce Meadows, and the Dutch government sends over four tonnes of freshly-cut flowers to decorate the grounds for Holland Day during the Masters competitions.

Annually Spruce Meadows sponsors Equi-Fair, North America's largest trade show for horse products. The big attractions, however, are the three spectacular riding competitions held each year.

The National, *early June*
The National starts the competitive year at Spruce Meadows. The tournament features the Canadian Show Jumping Championship. Among the highlights are the Shell Cup Derby and the Royal Bank World Cup.

The North American, *during the first week of July*
The North American attracts riders from across the continent and climaxes with the North American Championship. Featured competitions include the Chrysler Classic Derby and the Queen Elizabeth II Cup.

The Masters, *early September*
The Masters ends the season with a sensational show. With prize money approaching $1.5 million, it offers the largest prize for show jumping in the world. It commences with a Parade of Competitors that can stretch more than a kilometre long and include more than 200 horses. As many as 11 countries are

Spruce Meadows

Competitions at Spruce Meadows feature the finest equestian athletes in the world

represented in the Amoco Festival of Nations during the Masters. Featured events include the du Maurier Ltd. International and the Bank of Montreal Nations' Cup. Friday evening, during the Masters, is devoted to the Canadian Airlines' Evening of the Horse, which includes the $50,000 Canadian Airlines Challenge.

Although competitions are held on only a few days each year, visitors are always welcome during regular office hours. There is always something to see—the beautiful grounds, horses in training, a well-appointed tack shop and souvenir store.

To the Southern family and everyone else who loves horses, it's a dream come true.

For information, call 974-4200.

International attraction began as family hobby

9. Northwest

Birds have adapted to life in the city

You may search in vain for the Kensington district on your average street map. Kensington is more an attitude than an address. It exists in places both on, and considerably off, the busy avenue known as Kensington Road NW. The best way to explore the area is on foot. You'll know

you've arrived in the North-west social hotspot when the scent of freshly-ground coffee wafts out the door of almost every shop you pass.

Kensington is hip and cool. Kensington is alternative and new age. Kensington is coffee.

Technically, the community is mostly in Hillhurst and partly in Sunnyside. But Kensington has never paid much mind to technicalities. Its bridge across the Bow, a bridge of graceful arches, is one of Calgary's most beautiful. Though formally named the Hillhurst Bridge, Kensington calls it the Louise Bridge.

And who was Louise?

That's a Kensington mystery. The best contender for the honor seems to be Queen Victoria's daughter, Princess Louise Caroline Alberta, who also had a province, a town, and a famous lake named after her.

Louise's pretty bridge, built in 1921 and restored in 1995, is the best starting point to explore Kensington. From there, the district ambles north up 10th Street as far as Riley Park, historic site of Calgary's only hippie love-in during the summer of 1967. From 10th, it rambles west along Kensington Boulevard up to 14th Street NW and strays east

along 3rd Avenue for a few blocks.

At the intersection of the two main arteries, 10th and Kensington, you will feel the Kensington heartbeat. Nearby is one of Western Canada's most whimsical toy stores, and around the corner is an esteemed repertory cinema. There are a couple of good bookshops, record stores, an abundance of boutiques, and almost enough cappuccino to satisfy the thirst of every Calgarian.

Kensington has a long and noble tradition of being in the cultural vanguard. For decades it has been the haunt of art

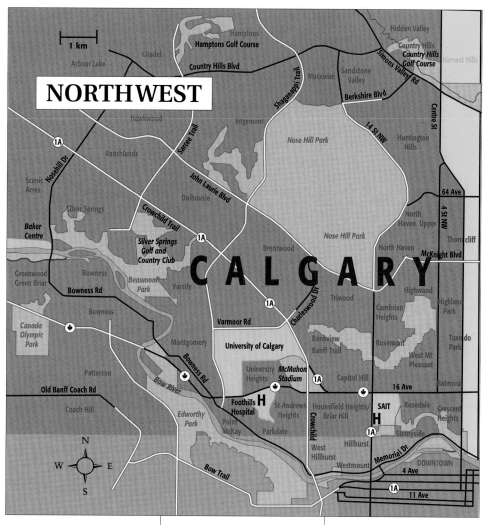

NORTHWEST

1 km

Hamptons
Hamptons Golf Course
Citadel
Arbour Lake
Country Hills Blvd
Hidden Valley
Country Hills
Country Hills Golf Course
Harvest Hills
Simons Valley Rd
Macewan
Sandstone Valley
Shaganappi Trail
Berkshire Blvd
Centre St
Hawkwood
Edgemont
Sarcee Trail
Nose Hill Park
14 St NW
Huntington Hills
1A
Ranchlands
John Laurie Blvd
Scenic Acres
Nosehill Dr
Dalhousie
64 Ave
Silver Springs
Crowchild Trail
1A
North Haven Upper
4 St NW
Baker Centre
Silver Springs Golf and Country Club
Nose Hill Park
Thorncliff
Greenwood
Green Briar
Bowness
Beaumont Park
Varsity
Brentwood
North Haven
McKnight Blvd
C A L G A R Y
Bowness Rd
1A
Triwood
Highwood
Highland Park
Bowness
Varmoor Rd
Charleswood Dr
Cambrian Heights
Canada Olympic Park
Montgomery
Bowness Rd
University of Calgary
Bankview
Banff Trail
Rosemont
West Mt Pleasant
Tuxedo Park
Patterson
Bow River
University Heights
McMahon Stadium
1A
Capitol Hill
16 Ave
Balmoral
Old Banff Coach Rd
Foothills Hospital **H**
St Andrews Heights
Hounsfield Heights/ Briar Hill
SAIT
Rosedale
Crescent Heights
Coach Hill
Edworthy Park
Point McKay
Parkdale
Crowchild
H
1A
Sunnyside
West Hillhurst
Hillhurst
Westmount
Memorial Dr
4 Ave
DOWNTOWN
N
W E
S
Bow Trail
1A
11 Ave

students from the nearby Alberta College of Art. It has great bars, fashionable eateries, and Calgary's most startling retail architecture, especially the colorful Kensington Pointe flatiron-style building designed by architect and entrepreneur Dan Jenkins.

Unto the Hills

When Calgarians seek guidance, they head for the hills—and there they find some of the finest educational institutions in Canada: the Alberta College of Art (ACA), the Southern Alberta Institute of Technology (SAIT, often called "the Tech" by oldtimers), and the University of Calgary (U of C).

Virtually all of Calgary's great intellectual workshops are in the hills of the northwest quadrant. They flourish beneath the sheltering shoulders of Nose Hill. The notable exception is Mount Royal College, which is atop a windswept southwest plateau.

SAIT and the ACA stand dramatically atop the hill above Riley Park. SAIT started in 1916 as the Provincial Institute of Technology and Art. The oldest building on the campus is the picturesque Heritage Hall, which was built in 1921 and opened for classes in 1922. During the Second World War the campus was taken over by the Royal Canadian Air Force and converted into Wireless School No. 2.

Annual raft race comes to shore at finish line near Louise Bridge

Students from "the Tech" had to continue their studies at the Stampede Grandstand.

Today SAIT, which adopted its current name in 1965, has a total student population of roughly 30,000. Only 5,500 are full-time and the rest are part-time, taking courses in everything from welding and cooking to drafting and newspaper reporting.

The ACA is one of the largest art colleges in Canada. It attracts about 750 students each year. Areas of study range from the traditional artforms of painting and sculpture to the most avant-garde. The Illingworth Kerr Gallery at the college, which is named in honor of the famous painter who was college director for many years, is open to the public Tuesday to Saturday from 10 am to 6 pm.

Attached to the ACA is the Jubilee Auditorium, Calgary's largest concert hall. Like its identical twin in Edmonton, the Jubilee was built to commemorate Alberta's 50th anniversary as a province in 1955. It took two years to build and was opened in 1957. The Jubilee's main auditorium has 2,713 seats; downstairs there is the 200-seat Dr. Betty Mitchell Theatre as well as rooms for meetings and exhibitions.

The Bruce

In front of the Jubilee and the College of Art is Calgary's most dramatic equestrian statue, a massive monument depicting a knight on horseback.

He is no gentle playtime knight, jousting for my lady's favor. He is an axe-wielding warrior, a medieval master of mayhem and man-to-man combat. He is a leader who is willing to kill, or be killed, in defence of his principles.

Calgary's knight on horseback is Robert the Bruce. On June 24, 1314, The Bruce defeated England's Edward II and his army. The battle, a major turning-point of British history, was fought in a boggy valley bottom called Bannockburn. Edward's knights were mired in the bog. The Bruce charged from the high ground. The Scots attacked with spears and sent the English running. King Edward himself barely escaped.

Robert the Bruce is Calgary's most conspicuous link with Scotland, the land that gave Calgary its name. The statue was donated by the late Eric Harvie, a prosperous Calgary oilman who was inspired by his family's Scottish origins. Harvie's generosity was tempered by his pride. When the statue was put on the hillside in 1967, some art students held a rally to protest the site. They felt it would be better to put it downtown where more people could see it. Harvie was offended and canceled a series of art scholarships he had earlier established.

The statue of The Bruce was created by sculptor Charles d'O Pilkington Jackson and was cast in an edition of only two; then the mold was broken. The other casting was erected at Bannockburn and was unveiled by the Queen.

Scottish Arms

The University of Calgary honors the city's connection with Scotland in its academic pageantry. Formal academic robes are modeled after those used in Scottish universities. Also, the university's coat of arms was registered with the Lord Lyon King of Arms at Edinburgh, who governs the heraldry of the Scottish clans. The U of C motto, *Mo shuile togam suas*, is Gaelic for "I will lift up my eyes" and is taken from a Gaelic translation of Psalm 121.

Classes began on the U of C campus in 1960, at first as part of the University of Alberta, which is based in Edmonton. It wasn't until 1967 that the University of Calgary granted degrees of its own. Today the university has an enrollment of almost 17,000 — that's full-time. There are also 2,700 part-time, pursuing studies in all fields from electrical engineering and English literature to law and medicine.

On the campus are some of Calgary's finest sports facilities, including the Olympic Oval with speedskating track, pools, and gymnasiums. These are available to the public when students aren't using them. The U of C is also in charge of McMahon Stadium, even though the professional Stampeder Football Club uses it more than the U of C student team, the Dinosaurs.

Bowness Park

The district of Bowness once was a separate town well beyond the city limits of Calgary. However, right from the beginning in 1912, its major attraction, Bowness Park, was owned and operated by Calgary.

The park was intended to spur real estate development, but growth came slowly. It took decades before the vast fields of vacant lots in Bowness property were built up. All through the years, however, Bowness Park was a recreational jewel. Each summer thousands of Calgarians would take the long streetcar ride to Bowness and enjoy picnics or paddling about in rented ca-

Bowness Park canals are used for boating in summer, skating in winter

noes. In winter, the lagoons became the city's largest skating rink. Today, the streetcar has been replaced by buses and automobiles, but the canoes and the skating continue to make Bowness a choice destination.

John Hextall

JOHN HEXTALL was a dreamer of brief but beautiful dreams.

He set his eyes on Bowness. It's been part of Calgary for ages, but then Bowness was remote ranchland. Hextall dreamed the wild valley was inhabited by the wealthiest families in southern Alberta.

In Bowness, Hextall saw wide avenues leading to stately homes. The houses were palaces surrounded by elegant garden grounds. In 1908, such dreams seemed likely to turn in-to reality. Times were good.

Hextall brought his dream to life in 1910. He built a few grand houses and a golf course. He built a bridge across the Bow, now a monument to his memory. Then he donated Bowness Park to Calgary; in exchange, the city built a street-car line to the community in 1912.

An economic recession in 1913 stalled the dream. It ended forever in 1914. Hextall got frostbite on his nose; the resulting infection took his life.

The Nose

CALGARY'S MOST PROMINENT natural feature is Nose Hill. The top of the hill is now one of the city's newest and largest natural recreational areas, Nose Hill Park.

The native people, fur traders, and explorers had a simpler name for the towering promontory; for them, it was just The Nose.

It was one of the key landmarks in the region. Its height made it visible for a great distance in all directions. For thousands of years before highways, The Nose was a grand signpost. Travelers in search of water and green grass for their horses knew they could find it right under The Nose.

How it got its curious name is uncertain. Some researchers, such as historical novelist Rudy Wiebe, declare the name was inspired by an ancient legend about Napi or Old Man, the trickster deity of the native peoples of the prairies.

Others report early settlers were told by native elders that Nose Hill and nearby Nose Creek got their names because of a cruel punishment given to adulterous native wives. Apparently, their noses were slit or cut off by their husbands in rituals taking place near the creek.

Historian Hugh Dempsey is reluctant to believe either theory. He has been collecting Napi stories for forty years but has never heard any that involve Napi's nose—although he has gathered a multitude about other prodigious parts of Napi's anatomy. As well, he suggests settlers' accounts about native traditions are often unreliable. As for the al-

The haunting cry of the hawk is still heard on The Nose

leged nose-slitting, he says, "I think it would have been an isolated event."

Perhaps The Nose got its name because it *looked* like a nose to anyone who had been traveling for days across the flat prairies. It certainly stuck out. At its peak, The Nose is 230 metres above the valley below, making it a grand viewpoint to keep an eye on things in all directions.

To the native people who set up their teepees at the top, and who left dozens of teepee rings for archeologists to discover, The Nose was the equivalent of a luxury high-rise apartment tower. Along with the stupendous view, there was a ready supply of fresh spring water, plenty of food on the hoof in the buffalo grazing areas, and lots of tasty berries in the coulees. It was even air-conditioned. The cool hilltop breezes blew away mosquitoes and other insects infesting lower areas. It probably also had great significance for sacred ceremonies and other important social events.

Once the settlers arrived, The Nose was put to work. Cattle and

horses were set to pasture where buffalo had roamed. Large fields were plowed and sown with wheat, barley and hay. One area on the eastern edge was mined for gravel. Following close on the heels of farmers and ranchers came the real estate planners who wanted to develop every last square centimetre of The Nose.

In 1990, after more than two decades of contentious debate among developers, city council, and environmental activists, a total of 1127 hectares—a vast area but still only the topmost tip of The Nose — was set aside as a natural prairie grassland park. Environmental damage from earlier years is now being repaired and sensitive areas, including important native sites, have been protected.

Today, it still acts as a natural billboard—just as it did in the era of the buffalo hunters. Now, however, The Nose is a sign and symbol of untamed nature. Here, it says, are wild roses and crocuses, rabbits and porcupines, owls and free-flying hawks. The prairie paradise has not been paved.

U of C sculpture from 1988 Olympics is exactly 19.88 metres high

Cairn

WHERE IS THE University of Calgary?

The easy answer is that the U of C is located at the end of University Drive in Northwest Calgary. The campus is west of Crowchild Trail between 24th and 32nd Avenues NW.

But that wasn't good enough for U of C engineering professor Bill Teskey. He organized a project in 1988 to pin the campus down to a precise point. The project was to commemorate the centennial of professional engineering in Canada.

No other point on the face of the planet has been measured in so many ways. A cairn, positioned in front of the engineering complex, marks the place ac-

U of C's engineering monument

cording to all standard engineering parameters:

- astronomical latitude is 51 degrees 04 minutes 48 seconds North
- astronomical longitude is 114 degrees 07 minutes 55 seconds West
- Dominion Lands Survey location is LS14 - S30 - T-24 - R1 - W5
- height above sea level is 1,115.4 metres
- distance north of the equator is 5,626,394 metres
- distance from centre of the earth is 6,366,344 metres
- magnitude of gravity is 980,800.3 milligals
- mean distance to the moon is 384,000 km
- mean distance to the sun is 149,600,000 km

Northwest Restaurants

RESTAURANT CRITIC John Gilchrist's recommendations for the Northwest:

Naturbahn Teahouse, at Canada Olympic Park (247-5465), is only open for Sunday brunch, but it certainly has the best view of any restaurant in the city. At the top of the luge run, it serves good Germanic-style food.

In that veritable restaurant row of Motel Village, there's the **Louisiana House**, 2231 Banff Trail NW (289-3096), at the Avondale Motor Inn. It's a wonderful Cajun-style restaurant where you enjoy huge amounts of food for very cheap prices.

In the Kensington area, for a light lunch, there's the **Sweet Art Pastry Cafe**, 130 - 10th Street NW (270-8442), featuring fine baking, soup, and café au lait. On Northmount Drive is the **Puspa**, 1051 - 40th Ave NW (282-6444). Here you'll find excellent Indian cuisine and very nice people.

On Centre Street North is the **Santorini Taverna**, 1502 Centre Street N (276-8363), which is probably the best Greek restaurant in town. There is also a Vietnamese place called the **Trong Khanh**, 1115 Centre Street N (230-2408), serving the most food you'll be able to get for the buck anywhere in the city.

The **Moroccan Castle**, 217 - 19th Street NW (283-5452), is one of those sit-back-on-the-couch, eat-with-your-hands places with wonderful Moroccan cuisine. Further up 19th, there's the **Blue House Cafe**, 3843 - 19th Street NW (284-9111). It's a Caribbean restaurant and a good little place.

Canada Olympic Park

CANADA OLYMPIC PARK is where Calgarians go downhill fast—some of them faster than anyone else on the face of the planet.

COP, as most call it, is absolutely the finest ski and sleigh facility in the land. The world's best athletes competed there during the 1988 Olympic Winter Games. Now dozens of other competitions are held there each winter—and future champions are in training there on the ski slopes and sleigh runs.

During the '88 Winter Games, COP was where competitions were held for bobsleigh, luge, ski jumping and freestyle. The luge and bobsleigh runs are designed for international competitions and for training Canada's national teams, but the public is able to enjoy the descent. A short section of the luge track is available for the sport luger, even in the summertime.

Those wanting a longer and faster ride can take a trip with two members of a bobsleigh team, a professional driver and a brakeman. The bobsleigh plummets downhill at speeds of 120

Canada Olympic Park is a beacon for all winter sports athletes

km/h and twists its way through 14 turns and curves. Riders in groups can descend four at a time in the Bobsleigh Bullet, a specially-designed sled that needs no driver and has built-in brakes. The Bullet blasts its way downhill at 90 km/h and comes to a gentle stop by itself at the bottom.

Most visitors to COP, however, prefer to work their way to the bottom of the hill on their own two skis. The COP ski hill attracts 130,000 skiers each winter. The park is able to provide instruction for all types of skiing, from ski-jumping and downhill to cross-country and telemark. It is now the largest ski school in Western Canada.

The buildings and facilities at COP were built at a cost of $72 million by the federal government and are operated by the Canada Olympic Development Association (CODA). Special care was taken to fit the structures into the landscape. The outbuildings were painted in a variety of

farm and ranch colors. Now a buffer zone of willows and aspen poplars surrounding COP is being left as an undeveloped nature preserve.

COP is truly a beacon for Calgarians. The ski hill is brightly lit for night skiing. The entire hillside glows and can be seen shining in the night dozens of kilometres away. The 90-metre ski jump tower is the landmark that stands like a sentinel on the horizon. The tower is open for public tours. To get to the observation deck on top, take the glass-enclosed elevator. The view is impressive. To the east is Calgary, and to the west are the foothills and gleaming Rockies.

Skiers get a long season at COP, thanks to the extensive array of snow-making machinery on the ski hill. The slope is groomed daily to keep it in top condition. The luge and bobsleigh runs are kept well below the freezing point by a vast network of refrigeration equipment. Slippery plastic surfaces mounted

COP Facts

CANADA OLYMPIC PARK is located by the TransCanada Highway on the western edge of Calgary, 15 minutes drive from the city centre.

During the winter ski season, the ski hill is open from 10 am to 10 pm weekdays and from 9 am to 5 pm on weekends.

Ski registrations	299-0880
Bobsleigh rides	247-5490
Guest services	247-5452

Canada Olympic Park

Ski season at Canada Olympic Park is extended by sophisticated snow-making equipment

on some of the jumps allow skiers to keep in top form even on warm summer days.

The daylodge at COP includes rental facilities, cafeteria, pub, and ski shop. Attached to the daylodge is the Olympic Hall of Fame and Museum, which has exhibits tracing the history of the Olympic Winter Games from the very beginning.

During the summer, softball games and other activities are held at COP. The Olympic excitement continues year-round.

10. Northeast

Calgary's International Airport is administered by the Calgary Airport Authority as a community resource

The Northeast is Calgary's big front door. For all visitors arriving on wings, and for many who arrive on wheels, the Northeast is where they get those important first impressions of the city. Visitors traveling by air are welcomed at the Calgary International Airport, rated as the most

modern in Canada and, according to management policy, striving to be the most friendly as well.

Travelers coming by car or bus from the south and west have their own routes into the heart of the city, but most visitors traveling from the north or east will enter the city on either of the two busiest highways in the West, the Trans-Canada Highway, or the provincial Highway 2.

Highway 2 is the busiest route. Running north and south, it is the blacktop backbone of the province, the prime route linking Edmonton and Calgary, as well as most of

the major towns in the province. Within the city, Highway 2 is best known as Deerfoot Trail, and the Trans-Canada is identified as 16th Avenue North.

The fastest and most picturesque route from the airport to the downtown area is to take the Deerfoot, then turn onto Memorial Drive. It presents the city at its finest. The route is landscaped with vast tracts of green space, including two golf courses and other athletic parks, and it culminates in a series of spectacular glimpses of the downtown skyline.

Growth Area

There are a few neighborhoods in the Northeast that trace their history back to pioneer days, but most of the area was developed in recent decades. As a result, the Northeast has a more efficient transportation system than older sections of Calgary. As well, the shopping district is more varied. Many merchants in the Northeast set up shop in buildings designed to be warehouses. With the reasonable rents and ease of parking, the Northeast is a fertile growth area for bulk distributors as well as specialty shops. Many high tech industries have been

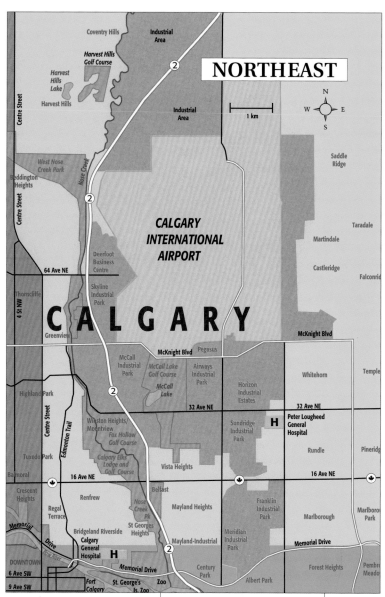

visit to the market. For many, cruising through the Crossroads looking for bargains is a form of recreation and relaxation.

Cultural Diversity

There are no ghettos in Calgary and no areas entirely occupied by a particular ethnic group. However, the Northeast does have a long tradition of the greatest cultural diversity of any section of the city. It began early in the century, when the Bridgeland-Riverside district was known either as Little Germany or Little Italy because of the number of people from those countries who had settled there.

Today, the tradition continues. The Northeast is home to a great influx of Calgarians who came from Asia, Europe, and Africa. They have established many restaurants that serve ethnic foods, shops that stock specialty items from "back home," as well as many outstanding churches and temples.

Aero Space Museum

It took the human race an

established near the airport to take advantage of the transportation and communication.

One of the most popular shopping districts is located on the TransCanada, near the intersection with Deerfoot in the district known appropriately as the Crossroads.

Tucked behind the Crossroads Hotel in a huge former warehouse is the Crossroads Market, Calgary's largest farmers' market and flea market. Here, everything is for sale, from fresh produce to second-hand auto parts and recycled home furnishings. Each weekend thousands of Calgarians pay a eternity to learn how to fly. The Wright brothers turned their bicycle shop into an aircraft factory to build their first plane. They made one short hop with it in 1903 and forever changed the way the world travels.

Calgary's Aero Space Museum, at the northwest corner of McKnight Boulevard and 19th Street NE, traces the footsteps of the Wright boys—and thousands of other historic aviators, from bush fliers to bomber pilots. The special focus is the story of aviation in Calgary.

The museum is housed in one of the few airport hangars left over from the Second World War. The hangar is crammed with plane parts, equipment, and tools. Rare historic engines from the first decades of flight are arrayed on racks, almost as if they were on an assembly line. Hanging from the rafters are exhibits in various stages of restoration. And in the air is the scent of the "dope" painted onto the fabric of cloth-covered wings.

The Aero Space Museum has a great wealth of priceless aircraft, many of which are desperately in need of tender loving care. It's a big job and requires great attention to detail. With a crew of dedicated volunteers and craftsmen hired on short-term government employment grants, the plan is to build one of the largest fleets of vintage planes on the continent.

The museum is remarkably generous with its exhibits. Some of the finest examples are on loan to other institutions. Three of the museum's

Even the happiest family outings must come to an end

best-restored fighter planes are on display at the Naval Museum of Alberta in Southwest Calgary. As well, hanging dramatically from girders in the entrance foyer of the PetroCanada Centre is the museum's bright yellow Noorduyn Norseman, a plane very popular with early bush pilots who flew Calgary geologists to oil discoveries in the Far North.

The greatest challenge facing the restoration crew is the museum's largest plane, the Avro Lancaster. The Lanc was one of the most effective bombers of the Second World War and was the type of plane used during the famous "dam busters" raids. The museum's Lanc, however, was manufactured in 1945 and was never flown in active battle. It came to Calgary in 1962 and was set on a pedestal at the airport as a war memorial.

Unfortunately, the plane was damaged on the pedestal by vandals and weather. In

1992 the Lanc was removed from the pedestal and moved to the nearby museum, where it awaits a thorough restoration.

The museum is open from 10 to 5 weekdays and from 11 to 5 on weekends.

International Airport

Calgary's airport is profoundly important to the city and the region. It's as important as the waterfront is to a seacoast city. It's one of the most significant transportation centres on the continent. The Calgary International Airport has the longest runway of all civil airfields in Canada and has the largest fleet of corporate aircraft in the country.

The current terminal building was opened in 1977. At that time it was administered directly by the federal government. In 1992, after many years of negotiations, the airport was transferred to a local organization, the Calgary Airport Authority. The Authority has made the terminal much more of a people place by improving the facilities and adding an array of shops and services.

Calgarians are proud of their airport. Probably the proudest are the 75 members of a group called the White Hat Welcome Hosts. These volunteers, dressed in white hats and red vests, are on hand during all the busiest hours to welcome visitors from foreign lands. The volunteers, many of them retired, also conduct tours for school children, service clubs, and other community associations.

Calgarians have always been at the forefront of aviation in Canada. The earliest experimental flights in Calgary were conducted in 1911, just eight years after the very first flight by the Wright brothers.

Calgary's first airport was a grassy field in the Bowness district. In 1928, a new site was selected in Southwest Calgary in what is now Wildwood. However, turbulent winds there made it difficult for planes to land safely, so the airport was moved to the Northeast in what is now Renfrew district. The Renfrew site was used until 1939, when the current airport was

opened for service.

Calgary was one of the earliest cities to be served by Canada's first major airline, Trans Canada Airlines (TCA, now Air Canada). The airline began scheduled flights to and from Calgary in 1939. Now the International Airport is used by nine airlines carrying passengers around the world.

Northeast Restaurants

RESTAURANT CRITIC John Gilchrist's recommendations for the Northeast:

Calgary's best burgers are at **Boogie's Burgers**, 908 Edmonton Trail NE (230-7070. Such a funny place—but good burgers.

Up on 32nd Avenue is **Nirvana Kitchen**, 1935 - 32nd Avenue NE (291-0445), which has excellent Punjabi style cuisine.

The Spruce Goose Cafe, 1441 Aviation Park NE (295-4140), is in the flight centre and has a glass wall so patrons can watch the airplanes come and go. Offering a menu which reflects a Danish influenced, it also provides food service for private airplanes. A great little cafe, it's excellent for a Sunday brunch, especially if you've got the kids. They'll like to watch the airplanes.

Mario's, 3220 - 5th Avenue NE (248-7070), is a great Italian restaurant with nice people.

For a cool treat, try **Confetti Ice Cream**, 4416 - 5th Street NE (277-5731). They serve good stuff.

David Dover

DAVID DOVER is the son of former alderman Mary Dover and the great-grandson of Col. James Macleod, who named Calgary. He is a private pilot, past-president of the Calgary Chamber of Commerce and is Chairman of the Calgary Airport Authority which administers the airport as a community resource.

We're very public in the way we operate. We tell everybody what we're doing. We publish our financial results; we have meetings with service clubs. The city council actually holds meetings there. We talk to the caucuses of all the political parties. We have a very large contingent of what we call stakeholders, the

people who actually operate at the airport, and they're part of our planning process.

Our first constituent is the traveling public. What we've got to do is deliver the lowest possible cost to the traveling public, and we've been able to do that. I think we're the lowest cost facility for the air carriers in the system.

We rewrote the contracts with all of our tenants to ensure the prices they charged for the food and the other items that are sold are not one cent more than what they could get off-airport. We don't rip people off because they're at the airport.

Reference

The best resources for the student of Calgary history are in the library and archives at the Glenbow Museum and in the Local History Room at the main branch of the Calgary Public Library.

Artiss, Laurie, ed. *Pin Collectors Guide to the 1988 Calgary Winter Olympic Winter Games.* Dominion Sports Marketing, 1988.

Barraclough, Morris. *From Prairie to Park.* Century Calgary Publication, 1975.

Beaty, Chester B. *The Landscapes of Southern Alberta: A Regional Geomorphology.* Lethbridge: University of Lethbridge, 1975.

Belanger, Art J. *A Half Mile of Hell: The Story of Chuckwagon Racing.* Frontier Books, 1970.

Birrell, Dave, and Ron Ellis. *Calgary's Mountain Panorama.* Rocky Mountain Books, 1990.

Bott, Robert. *The University of Calgary: A Place of Vision.* The University of Calgary Press, 1990.

Bovey, Robin. *Birds of Calgary.* Revised and expanded edition. Lone Pine, 1990.

Bullick, Terry. *Calgary Parks and Pathways.* Rocky Mountain Books, 1990.

Burns and Elliott, eds. *Calgary, Alberta, Canada: Her Industries and Resources.* 1885. Reprint edition. Glenbow, 1974.

Carroll, Norma, ed. *The Heritage Park Story.* Heritage Park, 1976.

Dempsey, Hugh A., ed. *The Best of Bob Edwards.* Edmonton: Hurtig, 1975.
———. *The Wit and Wisdom of Bob Edwards.* Edmonton: Hurtig, 1976.
———. *Calgary: Spirit of the West.* Glenbow and Fifth House, 1994.

Elphinstone, Dave. *Inglewood Bird Sanctuary — a place of all seasons.* Rocky Mountain Books, 1990.

Evans, Simon M. *Prince Charming Goes West: The story of the E.P. Ranch.* University of Calgary Press, 1993.

Foran, Max, and Shelagh S. Jameson, eds. *Citymakers: Calgarians After the Frontier.* Historical Society of Alberta, Chinook Country Chapter, 1987.

Fraser, W.B. *Calgary.* The Calgary Public School Local of the Alberta Teachers' Association, 1967.

Gard, Robert E. *Johnny Chinook: Tall Tales and True from the Canadian West.* New edition. Hurtig, 1967.

Gowans, Bruce W. *Wings Over Calgary 1906-1940.* Chinook Country Chapter, Historical Society of Alberta, 1990.

Hallworth, Berylm, ed. *Nose Hill: A Popular Guide.* Calgary Field Naturalists' Society, 1988.

Javorski, Mary. *The Canadian West Discovered.* Glenbow Museum, 1983.

Kennedy, Fred. *Alberta Was My Beat: Memoirs of a Western Newspaperman.* The Albertan, 1975.

Kwasny, Barbara, and Elaine Peake. *Look at Calgary's Art.* City of Calgary, 1977.

MacEwan, Grant. *Eye Opener Bob: The Story of Bob Edwards.* Edmonton: Institute of Applied Art, 1957.

McNeill, Leishman. *Tales of the Old Town.* [Calgary Herald, n.d.]

Peach, Jack. *Days Gone By.* Saskatoon: Fifth House, 1993.
———. *Thanks for the Memories: More Stories from Calgary's Past.* Saskatoon: Fifth House, 1994.

Pole, Graeme. *Classic Hikes of the Canadian Rockies.* Altitude, 1994.

Provost, George R. *Calgary 100: Calgary Centennial Souvenir Book.* Provost Promotions & Publications, 1974.

Robertson, Anna. *A Guide to Fish Creek Provincial Park.* Rocky Mountain Books, 1991.

Sheils, Bob. *Calgary.* Calgary Herald, 1974.

Sherrington, Peter, ed. *Calgary's Natural Areas: A Popular Guide.* Calgary Field Naturalists' Society, 1975.

Smith, Donald B. *Centennial City: Calgary 1894-1994.* University of Calgary Press, 1994.

Sparks, Susie, ed. *Calgary: A Living Heritage.* Junior League of Calgary, 1984.

Stenson, Fred. *The Story of Calgary.* Saskatoon: Fifth House, 1994.

Index

Photo Credits

HISTORICAL IMAGES

Glenbow Archives: 22, 26, 27, 28, 29, 31, 36, 40b, 42, 43, 64, 74, 101, 106a&b, 115b

CONTEMPORARY IMAGES

Alberta Tourism: 46-47
Angus of Calgary: 80b
Big Rock: 96a-b, 97
Ward Cameron: 76a
Barry Ferguson: 33
Calgary Stampede: inset front cover, 84-85, 87
Calgary Airport Authority, 120
Frozen Motion: 12, 34b, 45c, 58, 93
Glenbow Museum: 62, 63b&c
Gold Photography: 75
Maura Hamill: 90
Al Harvey: 119
Stephen Hutchings: 16-17, 39a, 111a&b
Bill Marsh: 65, 78-79, 80, 82, 83a, 86, 87a
Mathieson Photo Service Ltd.: 123
Ricardo Ordónez: 107, 108a, 112
Mike Ridewood: 92
Joe Scanlon: 89
Dennis Schmidt: 19a, 25
Esther Schmidt: 13, 14, 15b, 20, 21
Laurie Skreslet: 35
Take Stock Inc.: 2, 7, 10, 24, 37a, 38, 39b, 40a, 44, 50a, 52-53, 56, 60b, 61, 73, 88, 94, 98, 102a&b, 103b, 115a, 118
Patrick Tivy: 83, 114
George Webber: front cover, 6, 15a, 18-19, 103a, 122, bottom back cover
Deidre Williams: 8, 23, 32a&b, 34a, 35a, 37b, 41, 45a, 48, 50b, 51, 54, 55, 59, 60a, 63a, 66, 67a&b, 68, 69, 70, 71, 72, 76b, 77a&b, 81a-b, 95a&b, 104-105, 105a, 108b&c, 109, 116, 117a&b, top back cover

Acknowledgements

Inspiration and information for this book was generously provided by dozens of Calgarians, and to them, I give great thanks. I am especially grateful to Bruce Patterson for introducing me to Stephen Hutchings and his crew at Altitude.

Thanks to: Mairi Babey, Ken Bendiktsen, Valerie Berenyi, Jill Bergman, Robert Bott, Brian Brennan, Heather Bruce, Bernard Callebaut, Doug Cass, Danny Copithorne, Cheryl Dalik, Arthur Darby, Cathy Davidson, Hugh Dempsey, Paul Diemert, Kathy Dolan, David Dover, Sonya Dueck, Dave Elphinstone, Marianne Fedori, Tom Glass, Robert Graham, John Gilchrist, Michele Green, David Gurofsky, Maura Hamill, Claire Hamonic, Tom Head, Cherry Holand, Dan Hong, Janet Kuzik, Fae A. MacDonald, Jennifer MacLeod, Edward McNally, Isabella Miller, David Parker, Janet Pieschel, Candace Savage, Gladys Serafino, Laurie Skreslet, Donald B. Smith, Betty Jo Stauch, Dan Sullivan, Thomas Tait, Fred Valentine, Dirk Van Wyk, Laurie Wallis, Lynette Walton, Elizabeth Wesley, and Carla Yuill.

Special thanks go to my family for their unfailing support, especially my parents, former Calgarians Pat and Mary Tivy of Nanaimo, my daughters Jessica and Robin, and my wife Valerie Boser.

The Author

Patrick Tivy

Patrick Tivy was born in Calgary and is an alumnus of the University of Calgary. He has worked as copy editor, reporter, and columnist for both *The Albertan* and *Calgary Herald* newspapers, and as contributor to many magazines. This is his first book.